NADJA
THE PEARL OF SINJAR

by

Barbara Davis White

Copyright © 2018 BARBARA DAVIS WHITE
All rights reserved.
ISBN:1985740362
ISBN-13:978-1985740365

For my dear Mother, Rose Hershkovitz, who rests in Heaven, you taught us what "Loving ALL People" really means….

AMEN

DEDICATION

This book is dedicated to the wonderful Yezidi men, women and children, in Kurdistan, Northern Region of IRAQ, who suffered the horrendous atrocities by a group known to the modern world as ISIS. It is hard to comprehend in this day and time that the world would stand by and allow such destruction to human lives, but tragically it happened.

I would like to dedicate this work to my wonderful family who have been so patient with my moving and working in Kurdistan. I love you Tony, Solange, Amaris, Amir and Jency Davis! God Bless you. I have only hoped that through my small contribution all of our lives have been made sweeter.

LifeBridge Ministry, and all of those who support your work, Mike and Terri Taylor, there are no real words that can describe the love and support that you have poured out for those here in Kurdistan. Your strength and courage lie in your passion for fulfillment through community, family, hopes and dreams of a better future through Our Lord and Savior, Jesus Christ!

Kurdistan your kindness to all of the different cultures and religions have captured my heart. Your love and acceptance for the surviving Yezidi refugees is beyond admirable. You have literally sacrificed everything to help those who have lost everything.

To those who will take time to read this account...Thank You. Your time and concern means so very much.

Please keep in mind, that what affects even the remotest culture, has an effect on us all. Thank you to the precious women, men, boys and girls, for your courage to speak out, and tell your story to a world who is now waiting to hear.

So with that said, please take out your readers, your kleenex and your your love for a people who were not...and now they are!

AUTHOR'S NOTE

With the exception of the names, all of the incidents in this book are true. Each character written about will show the best and the worst of humanity. Each word here has been written through tears.

The history of the Region cannot be contained here in words as it is to vast and yet, it is where all eyes will ultimately be focused.

For each woman who has suffered abuse in any form, my heart goes out to you. Each man who has desired to work and change our volatile world, may you have the strength and courage of a lion.

For all who seek to forgive and go on, this book is for you.

Final note is that ALL proceeds from the sales of this book will go to the Dream Center to help educate the broken, wounded and those who dare to DREAM of a new future.

With Love,

Barbara Davis White

"Oh, if only I had the wings like a dove!

I would fly away and be at rest"

Psalm 55:6

CONTENTS

	Acknowledgments	i
1	Broken	1
2	The Yezidis	22
3	The Invasion of Sinjar	63
4	Mayhem	93
5	Living Hell	104
6	Mayan	141
7	The Escape	174
8	Amir	183
9	Elza	212
10	The Beginning	231

ACKNOWLEDGMENTS

There is nothing that we can ever accomplish without the concerted efforts of many special people, those seen and those unseen. Kurdistan you have my heart, forever.

First of all Jesus Christ, King of the Kingdom of God, Thank you for teaching us humanity as humans. We have no clue!

Special Thanks to Mohammed Suleiman Ahmed who has walked me through the history of the Kurdish People, and the wonderful Heritage that is shared through the faithful and brave Peshmerga. You have given me hours and even days of insight on life here in Kurdistan. It is because of you that I have a fruitful perspective and a heart filled with hope for the future. The Peshmerga are my Heroes Forever!

To all the precious students who have come through the Dream Center, you have filled my life with so much joy. Kurdish, Yezidi, Muslim, Iraqi, Christian, and Syrian. You have given my life such meaning.

Special Thanks to Life Bridge Ministries, Tree of Life, Rock Church, and Faith Christian Center for all of your love and prayers.

Kathy Barnett, a Fox News Contributor, your love for Jesus, Prayer and Fasting have enriched my walk. My friend and great contributor to the news from day to day in this volatile Region, Nick Contompasis, my heart is overwhelmed with how you love and support the United States of America and Kurdistan by speaking out for Justice.

I love you Sue and Victor McGill for always opening up your home and hearts to me. Vicki and Ronald Kessler, Barbara Burley, John and Kandi Harrington, Deborah Milford, Tracy Grieves, and Larry and Donna Nelson, thank you for your ongoing support.

Dr. Paul Martin Kingery, your work in Sege and even the preceding excerpts from your writings, speak for themselves. Thank you! Noel and Charlie you are my heartbeat here in Kurdistan.

Phillip B. Calhoun and Donna Sheron you have literally kept Yezidi children alive through your efforts in Sege. God Bless you and keep the fires burning.

Caleb and Paige Crawford (along with Baby Kye) you gave up everything to move here to Kurdistan and make a difference. And a great one you have made. Be Blessed in Erbil.

There are far too many people here who have made this book and work possible to thank, but just know that I love and pray for you all, both in America and abroad.

FORGIVENESS IS UNLOCKING THE DOOR….

AND FINDING OUT THAT YOU WERE

THE PRISONER.

MAX LUCADO

CHAPTER ONE
"BROKEN"

" There is no greater agony than bearing an untold story inside you."

Maya Angelou

A morbid silence filled the corridor where Nadja lay reclining. She was exhausted from either pacing or sitting broken in one place. She was exhausted just trying to take her next breath. Each man's sexual cruelty and beatings had left their mark. She shared the knowledge of the pains of a wounded animal whose chest rose and lowered waiting for death.

Yet, the stillness brought about a comfort that offered a mix of fear and hopefulness. She had deemed her sweet hopes and dreams of her past null and void. They had only served as painful reminders of what was never to be. She had grown tired of trying to fight the afflictions of such abuse.

No one could begin to imagine the horrors of not only watching, but experiencing first hand what it was like to be a child playing in the mountains one day, and then to be a sex slave the next. To be the recipient of any form of kindness had her in a confused state after being the object of hellish affections.

She had persistently reoccurring visions of her mother, sister and brothers, again and again. She thought that this would be her cursed, repetitive pattern for days and years to come.

No relief from the cold chains that stole her innocence. One day she was a little girl playing and dreaming and the next day she was tied up and blindfolded, in hopeless and disgusting world. Her family was destroyed in what seemed to be an instant.

Nadja was now very old for her 16 years of life. And that birthday was spent with several rapists having at her body, one after another. She had been forced to become a stranger to even to the girl that she thought she knew so well; herself.

She had no point of reference. Her family was gone, except for the brief, happy memories that she could not afford herself the luxury to call upon. Nadja was among the walking dead from the ravages of religious hostilities.

The rough edges of her blistered life were smoothed by her dynamic feminine presence. Although, she had lost any reason to smile, she still possessed the carved features of an angel. There was no denying that she still had the existing shards of residue that comes with being robbed of one's innocence, she refused to act as a weak and battered captive. Her teeth were stained, her skin was caustic and dry, and her long brown hair had become listless. The obvious results were visible of not recently having access to good care or hygiene.

Yet, her long dark brown hair framed her face. Her bright green eyes glowed like soft lamps in a warm old library in an English village manor. Her inner strength was apparent, and made it hard to determine if she was finding peace, or fighting a silent battle.

Undoubtably, the demons that had been left behind and who tormented her day and night were still raging. Yet, her head was so tenderly and regally held high. Her natural elegance elevated her demeanor above the damages that ISIS had inflicted.

Alarms of fear and hatred were so deep that they vibrated with fire in her young bones. Nadja was brought here after more than a year she had been taken from her village. She had been discovered wandering. She was found, thirsty and incoherent. One look at her and the Peshmerga Troops, from the area, had immediately known her plight.

They insisted that she had held a little branch and had swung it like a knife for over two hours while they tried to calm her. It now seemed like an eternity ago since she was introduced to those kind eyes of that certain Peshmerga Soldier. He had spotted Nadja, cared for her, and then carried her to a place of safety. be alive.

She had been found so dirty and scared, and still somewhere deep inside, regardless of the sadistic violations, she was somehow grateful to even be alive. She would for his sake try to pull herself out of the inauspicious pit of depravity and disappointment.

Even so, Nadja remained emotionless among those she resided with in the care facility. All the patients were like the walking dead from the results of the trauma and ravages of religious hostilities. She had been immobilized through the events that claimed her sanity and hopes.

The alarms of fear and hatred were so deep that they vibrated with fire in her young bones. She would let those alarms sound but she was not about to surrender to them, as she had never surrendered to ISIS even when the most horrific tortures were introduced to her young tender body.

As she sat each day there was nothing to do but revisit the relics of her past. They were always on standby. Nadja just remembered her village before the outrageously evil ISIS soldiers took their families away and discarded them like old trash.

Nadja's village of Sinjar had been invaded and destroyed. Every person had been left to defend themselves, killed or taken away by ISIS.

She was brought here to this facility from her new home. She had escaped and hoped to find a brand new family. She had escaped the horrors of hell. They had told her later that she had stayed in Sege wrapped in the arms of a Christian woman who was trying to help Yezidi refugees. She could not even remember the rescue or wandering into their village.

Nadja was now trying to grasp what was real and what was forced into her tender and defiled consciousness. Her new surroundings were beautiful and fit for a queen. The room was painted a pale but luscious green, with a soft beige trim. Every square inch kept reinforcing the thoughts of a new life that had the potential to spring forth.

She had a little dining table with four elegant pink and green cushioned chairs. This was for company so that she didn't always have to have meals alone. The windows were big and could be opened to allow the clean German fresh air to fill her room. The draperies were a soft ivory spiraling down along the sides of the big bay windows.

Yet, she kept them tightly closed for her own mental protection. She either wanted to jump out and flee, or she constantly imagined ISIS militia ascending the high walls, entering her room, and taking back their escaped goods. She pulled the curtains closed, and kept the windows covered so that she could faintly see out, but no one could see in.

Nadja had tried to insulate herself from the world between her new fresh linens. She continued to cling to her thick, soft white down comforter. She didn't want to come out ever again, not even to be restored.

She just wanted to hide for eternity with no one asking her questions. She didn't want to try to put into words her sordid recent past. She tried desperately to cover her head and face. Her whole body was shaking partially from the storm outside, and also from the inner storm that had churned like vomit within her soul.

She had never, ever not shared a room with someone before, and she felt even more alone. Her little sister had been her joy each morning for several years, and she believed in her heart of hearts, that she would not see that precious smile again. Not only would that little smile allude her, but so would the arms of her mother, who had left her without even one goodbye.

She hoped that it would soon begin to break. This place was new to her and it would take many days to get used to her new surroundings. To hear the rains pelt against her window made the days far more bleak, and she was having trouble seeing beyond her darkened skies as it was.

To add to her trauma she was now bleeding everyday. She would have to live with the molestations, the physical pain, and the horrible memories of loneliness and hunger. Except for the moments during her miraculous escape, she could not think of any reason to keep on living. So many women had already taken their own lives.

Nadja thought in her mind, however, that the physical injuries due to the rapes, and pains from the beatings could prove much easier to heal, than the mental abuse and loss of her family that she had endured. The wounds were so deep that she did not think that there was any remedy that could reach to their depth. Longing just to find some cloak of safety and protection, Nadja remained motionless and absorbed in her distress.

Suddenly, a caregiver's translator was gently whispering into Nadja's ear in Kurmanji Kurdish. This was the musical language of her beloved village. Oh, how she missed Mount Sinjar, or Shingal as it is sometimes referred to. She had heard the soft sounding voice mixed with the pouring rain outside of her window. It was even beginning to hail and there seemed to be no end to the torrential rains in Germany.

"May I get you **anything**, Nadja?" The voice was welcoming enough as it had tones of pleasantries, and it had interrupted her nightmares and daymares for just a brief moment. What does "anything" mean these days, she thought to herself? That was not a fair question. The inquiry implied that there was something that could be easily attained that could comfort her shattered heart.

It seemed to suggest that there was some mysterious elixir or words that could fill her with new life. She had so desired to toy with the hope and anticipation that somehow someone could enable her to walk out her days, but unfortunately the question was offered to a young woman whose heart was void of trust and expectation.

Nadja wanted to scream out, "leave me alone", but her voice would not cooperate on such a gloomy morning. She could not make the connection that she was in a new place designed to start her on a new journey of wholeness. She was in a million pieces that someone else held in their dirty hands. How would she even be able to begin a journey to heal?

This would be only to some degree and by degrees, however. She had been an object and anything that she had desperately need had not only been denied, but in the process she was mocked by men who took sport in handing out punishments just for asking. Oh, how they had taken great pleasure in making sure each girl was subject to their unpredictable behaviors.

Nadja was so confined to the horrors of her dishonored existence that she could not even bear to look in the mirror to wash her face. She hadn't seen her own face for over a year. ISIS had made sure of this. That sweet face, scarred and scared seemed to belong to someone else that she didn't know.

She would not meet the caregiver's eyes, but Nadja knew in fact that, Elza, her assigned caregiver had meant well. Why would she be there for any other reason? The lives of these women were in devastation yet, Elza was a kind German lady who had a light about her that Nadja could not identify.

Nadja had seen a cross hanging from the neck of Elza, but she had seen crosses before. She did not know if this implied that Elza bore her Christianity as a nominal symbol or as a deep belief. Her actions as she gave undivided attention to the women who were suffering in the care facility, seemed to suggest the latter.

Elza had a job to do, but she seemed intent on going way above and beyond her calling in this particular vocation. Nadja could call on her anytime of the day or night as Elza had been assigned to look after her.

She was selfless, and although there was a deep hurt in Elza's eyes, she was working feverishly with the broken women and children who had come into the program. It was a program by and for an organization specifically designed for Yezidi girls.

Nadja had witnessed such a deep compassion flowing through Elza's voice, but then there was also a mysterious inner strength that tugged tenderly at the heart strings of a reluctant Nadja. She would be forced out of the deep pit of what human cruelty had tossed her into whether she liked it or not.

This was Elza's mission to those who were so violently broken and wounded. She desired to see Nadja rise like a phoenix out of the ashes of despair. This would happen through the Grace of God, if Elza had anything to do with it.

These women and children had been stolen from their families by ISIS. They had been sold into sex slavery, and some of the girls had been as young as three years old. Mothers were captured right along with their daughters, but often times spilt up and sent to different towns and military compounds to be treated as sexual property and then sold or discarded by other methods.

The Christians and other Yezidi families had recently welcomed Nadja into their small village of Sege. She would try to start life over. This is the village where she had fled to catch her breath, and to pinch herself over and over, reminding herself that she was still alive. So many others would not be able to start again.

Nadja did not know if this was a blessing or a curse. She was mentally lost, but the love and help had flowed straight to her heart. That was the sacred reality of this little village and to the Yezidi People who had already arrived there. All were war torn, confused, scared and battered. The onslaught of her village being invaded, destroyed and inhabited by ISIS was almost more than she could bear.

Many UN Agencies came to Kurdistan to try and help the internationally displaced people find places to resettle their lives. They could never have imagined what they were walking into this time. Nadja was "discovered" in this village called Sege by an American group who lived, worked and dedicated every waking moment to helping the displaced and wounded find some sort of healing.

People would allow these gentle Americans and workers from several other countries into their painful lives to plead for some kind of humanitarian assistance. Women who weren't taken by ISIS now had no husbands or older sons to care for them. Many had taken in children who were not even theirs , but orphans in the recent invasion.

Some Americans even moved their families to assist in working tirelessly in attempting to keep the channels open to doctors and other workers sent in through a specific non-governmental organizations to seek out women just like herself.

These wonderful and dedicated workers had wanted to aid with provisions for the restoration of hers and many other souls. People and resources were limited in this aspect, but she was chosen to go to Germany, seeking help and hoping to detach from her terrible ordeal.

These caregivers were handpicked to tenderly to unwrap the painful layers of losing family, home and dignity. Each one of the people helping in the organization had their own story to tell. Elza's life had too been filled with trauma and violence, but she was an overcomer dedicated to helping others through their hideous ordeals. She was one remarkable woman.

Each individual who took part in seeing to it that the refugees who survived were remarkable people. There is no viable reward for caring for those who have lost family, friends and all earthly valuables, except seeing someone stand again after facing such horrible odds.

The people had to have housing, food, heaters with fuel, air-conditioning units to fight off the blistering heat of summer. They wanted to have some knowledge of where their loved ones had ended up and these workers would try to track some of their lost family.

At such a young age she was a perfect candidate to get ministry for her soul. There were teams of people waiting to try and restore some healing and wholeness to such a ravaged child.

In time, Elza would tell Nadja her painful story. She was extremely tender but showed no signs of being superficial. She did not patronize Nadja, but served her like she had been a captured queen.

The only reason that she could relate and empathize with the pains of so many others suffered in a more significant manner. She too had been there, although their stories of brutality were so extreme.

Her experiences were the stones on which to build lives again. Elza had fought back, and yet the memories were so vivid. She did not allow herself to dwell on the cards that had been handed to her in life, but played them with grace and courage.

However, Elza saw that Nadja's physical and emotional shock was so recent and brutal that she was going to have a very hard time adjusting to her new beginnings. She was so young and had been so innocent. She prayed that there would come a time that Nadja would feel compelled to grab onto some kind of anchor of help and hope.

Elza and the translators were wonderful people, but apart from a miracle, they could not shield her from the sordid memories of such evil predators. They had viciously taken up residence into her mind, heart and soul. This was not to mention the injuries that she had sustained in her body that would be impossible to treat even as time went by.

Nadja had no idea, upon her entering the clinic, that she had been blessed with one of the most conscientious people she would ever meet to help her begin a journey of healing.

So with the outside world going on as usual, in Germany, there were many women and children being treated in more than 20 clinics in Baden-Wuerttemberg, all set up and sanctioned by the Governor of that Region. The Yezidi, Christian and Shiite Muslim women were taken to these facilities.

These clinic have undisclosed locations with extra security out of fears that ISIS sympathizers may try to target them even in Germany. Nadja was now in one of these care facilities in a little German town. This was a clinic and trauma facility that was supposed to help destroy any memories that had violently fleeced her of her childhood.

None of these inflicted memories were hers but imposed and perpetrated on her by "human beings" who conducted life lower than any animal. She would be haunted by lingering nightmares that would continue to blacken her dreams for the rest of her life. This was her painful reality, but Nadja had kept forgetting that she was now in Germany.

Now the silence from the Arabic shouts by the hostile captors, no screams coming from the compound by the battered and abused girls, and the absence of horrible odors would take some time getting use to.

She could only picture the recent images of her past year that co-mingled with the beautiful thoughts that had surrounded her childhood. These were pictures that she did not want be reminded of. They were filled up by the invasion of not only their lives, but all future generations.She abhorred the thoughts of all these images. She longed to be empty, void of ALL recollections.

Coming from such a gruesome existence to peaceful surroundings was shocking in an of itself. The science and the serenity would take some getting used to. She lived in a shadow existence and now the light was blazing into her soul.

She had never been bothered by the rain before but the pounding and the fierce lightning and thunder only served to remind her of the night of chaos and disorder.

These were the sounds when ISIS took her family and friends away forever. These were the reminders of the cruel moments and the vicious people who had no hearts and killed every dream that had filled every life who had lived her village.

Inevitably, those who had escaped would be haunted forever by the screams and loved ones who could to get away. There was no escape from the torrential downpour of tears and the not so distant memories of relatives gone forever. She would instinctively reach for her little brother's curls to run her fingers through. But he was gone.

Her tortures were real and prevalent. So, also, as was the suffering and tragic plight of the other women and children who had arrived in this same clinic. Their accounts were also Nadja's. However, many of these women were so tortured, that they would be forever mentally and physically scarred with no return.

Now, she had found herself in what was worse than any bad dream. Nadja as well as the other women ate, drank and breathed their terrifying memories. She had been raped and beaten to the point that she was forced to become a stranger, even to the girl that she thought she had known so well; herself.

She had no point of reference for what had happened to her or what was to become of her in her empty existence. Her family was gone, except for the brief happy memories that she could not afford herself the luxury of pondering.

Memories of her hellish ordeal had wrestled their way into her dreams every night especially since entering this facility. It was quiet and with her new and peaceful environment, her unearthed inner corpses met her from morning until late at night. She saw the bloody scenes over and over in her mind.

She tossed and turned as she heard the reoccurring cries for help. She would put on 2 or 3 night garments to avoid the touch of anyone who may try and sneak into her room after the lights went out. She was hurting beyond anyone's imagination. Before each night was over she would vomit in her bed. The staff cleaned her up every morning, and there was not even a hint of disgust.

It had only been a short time that she was brought to the clinic, but now she now could urinate at will. During the times she was raped it was impossible. No one was watching her or dragging her down some dark corridor. The Arabic screams had ceased and she knew that it may be difficult, but not impossible to find a little peace.

It was still with hesitation she woke up day after day, knowing that there was some unknown reason she was kept alive but now she had to keep on fighting. It was a different battle, but survival is survival. She was scared and extremely angry that someone had this much control over her past and future. Yet, she knew that she had to somehow find a way to go on.

Strangely enough, her anger propelled her into facing each new sunrise. In order find answers, she would have to begin working on her own inward and complete transformation. She would not allow the animals to win. Nadja painfully accepted that she would have to touch all of the painful memories. The battle for her life was moment by moment.

Nadja had forced herself to think back. She had to face each moment of her frightful experience, and this is her story.

VICIOUS REMINDERS

The storm outside that had awakened her was fierce. This storm kept brewing from moment to moment, and the wind was howling like an injured animal that was trying to make it home to die. Oh, how she could relate. The thunder was very loud, and shook the entire room that she now inhabited.

Germany, this time of year, had sudden and frequent rain storms, but nothing could compare to the storm that was rattling the shutters of Nadja's mind. Was there anyone in her new world that could understand that she had not so long ago been the victim of nightly rapes and beatings, by numerous, brutal captors? She had been taken from her simple home and dominated by such hatred and violence that she could not foresee any chance of real recovery; full or even partial.

Nadja had been awakened by the imaginary sounds and smells of her recent ordeal. The torment lingered into her days from the nights of wrestling with demons real or imagined. She had been through more heartache than even those around her.

Then, Nadja was awakened every night by odd noises and she was having terrible night sweats. Her body shivered uncontrollably. Along with the pains from her being forcibly taken by ISIS, her family was all gone, and the cold had crept into her mornings now as as an undesirable intruder. In her mind she was unable to grasp the means and direction her heart should travel to have any sort of functional future.

Most spring mornings now were met with a rain which turned to soft pounding drops on the roof of her room. Nadja was from a totally different region in The Middle East, and she was not accustomed to the cool, damp mornings.

Shadows invaded her nights, and it was almost impossible to obtain any form of rest. It was not the clinic and those who were instrumental in this new arrangement. It was them. It was ISIS.

This clinic was formulated to initiate a healing process. Nadja could not even imagine any remedy for her woes. She was as fragile as well worn lace. Her memories had devoured her hopes, as they were still so fresh in her mind. She had been quickly transported to a new and unfamiliar place.

She had been meeting daily with the chosen care-givers who were capable of leading her out of this prison to a tiny bit of mental and physical calm. She would attempt to do her very best to cooperate.

She continued to wonder, "Who does these things to women and children? Who uproots and pillages whole valley villages and then murders their sons and fathers mercilessly? Who rapes young women for sport and then attempts to make themselves some kind of religious representative?

Who challenges every other belief system to uphold their own religion to the death? What warrants such beastly behavior?" Nadja had no answers only numerous questions that would plague her for the rest of her natural life.

She had to make a conscious effort just to continue to breathe, not to mention to formulate a life again from these horrible circumstances. Yet, from some unknown well there was a fountain softly flowing with waters of resurrection. Secretly, she knew that somehow she needed to begin to live again.

However, Nadja lived in two worlds. The heavy drops danced above her and reminded her that there were possibilities that there was still so much life to live. Her chains could be broken but it was going take some time.

Nadja did not feel like the woman that her captors had turned her into, but a helpless, small child and oh, how she longed for the arms of her mother, who was now dead.

She would have to dedicate each and every day of her life getting acquainted with her old self. However, regaining any sense of normalcy was going to be a steep mountain to climb. Her future had become her present, and vice versa.

Once on the slopes of recovery she knew that there would be no turning back. Where would she position these emotional and physical footings? She knew that she was called She was placed in the midst of a miracle assignment to conquer the painful step of healing.

There was a cold, cold breeze blowing through the huge open windows and the thick curtains were gently moving. Germany was lovely but so different.

Germany was where the peaceful streets were lined with blossoming trees. The rain made everything bloom, even Nadja eventually, but at such a high price. She would have to face her past. It was ever before her now. There was no escape. Not even here.

The pounding thunder shook the walls, and the noise just reminded her of the weapons and vehicles of the ISIS soldiers that darkened their village right before the invasion. Her village was once peaceful too.

Then, suddenly there were dark figures surrounding her village with massive amounts of vehicles and arms. The men wore black clothes and black head coverings, so as not to be recognized, but who could forget the filthy monsters as they spewed out orders to rape and kill innocent people.

Each day early in her arrival to the clinic, she had awakened more frightened and confused. On most new mornings she was in a complete state of partial paralysis. All of her attackers seemed to surround her in her imagination and the memories were changing and distorting themselves.

Nadja's dreams of her filthy captors were continuous and vivid, but to her relief, the dreams this time were interrupted by the pounding of the rain. The drenching rain made sounds to drown out the mental pictures. The flow of water sent a message of cleansing to her mind. It was almost the sound of peace.

She was mentally in chains in which there seemed to be no way of escape. Fears from her recent ordeal were being frantically triggered. Her new surroundings were still intimidating.

The little place in a small German town was where she had been taken for some elusive comfort and protection. Young Nadja had never been in a place which was by all accounts beautiful, but displayed signs of a clinical coolness. She had never even visited the village doctor.

The reflections of her short life distorted the picture of the scenes around the clinic like an impressionist artist's brush. Then there were sounds of traffic horns, and the other sounds that she could barely identify. They seemed to disturb her new found stillness, as she was still immersed in her recent dark chasm.

Nadja was in a completely foreign environment, and it was unfamiliar right down to the sights and smells. Everything was new including the food. She was from a small village where there was peace, although not lasting, in her home surrounded by the mountains. That was all she knew; her beautiful village in Kurdistan, IRAQ.

Nadja had been brought to Germany after more than a year of not just being abducted but she had not been sold to total strangers like the other girls. She was captured and made to dwell among the lowest of animals for a time that was too long in her short life.

For the most part, her new dwelling in Germany had been quiet and serene, but this time she could not help but to react to the pellets of sleet pounding against the roof of the building.

Only the smell of old urine and body fluids were burned into her memory. She had to remind herself every morning now that that she was in a safe place. She had a clean bed and at will she could lock and unlock her own door.

She was reminded of the bullets that murdered, mixed with the haunting screams of the women and young girls ripped away from their loved ones. These scenes were engraved so deep in her being that they played over and over again in her mind.

On one particularly raining and blustery morning, she had been pleasantly awakened by the sound of a piano playing faintly in another room. She was relatively new to this current state of living, and she suddenly realized that she had not heard music nor smelled flowers in over a year. Their fragrance filled the air. It was a heavenly refreshing mist that filled her nostrils.

However, the lock could not keep out the vivid horrors of the mental lens that scorched her consciousness. She wept every time the pictures produced themselves in her mind of her family and the fate that they had suffered at the hands of ISIS. The images of her family on the last day she that would see them whole, would haunt her for the rest of her life.

Nadja could not only hear the sound of the piano, but the sound of people singing and laughing, when someone hit a sour note. The people all laughed and continued to join in, even though it was early morning. She had been engulfed in the flames of hell for so long, she hadn't realized music or laughter any longer existed. It had been forbidden to her for over a year.

There was no celebration in the loss of all of her family and her friends. Her recent memories were only of the kidnappers screaming demeaning things to her and those only in Arabic. If she didn't understand the implied orders she was beaten...or worse, and she had the cigarette burns scarring her arms and legs to remind her of her insolence towards her captors.

No dancing, no weddings, except forced marriages, and certainly no more celebrations. ISIS was strict about joyless living. Each day of captivity offered no levity. No one was engaged in laughter unless it was used as a weapon to shame their tortured victims.

During her stay at the compound, psychological torture was real. This kept order if ISIS could maintain their threshold of fear. Many times she was awakened in the middle of the night and beaten for no reason, and the random acts of torture forced her to comply with their sick demands. They had kept her tired, weak, hungry and confused as a means of control, but that is how you conquer a human innocent soul.

Her life had become an enigma. The sights and smells seemed forever familiar. in her mind was the mental picture of the fixed gaze of the eyes of the dead. It was a dark drama mirrored by reality. It played on and on. The scenes fought her will to engage in her new found protection and care at the clinic.

However, Nadja still had no idea how to respond. She was in a lucid world of despair coupled with fear and shock. She was merely a shadow of herself drowning in a sea of confusion. Sleepless nights invaded by recollections that were echoes of her living death. Her constant struggle to want to keep breathing for any reason was met with tremendous effort.

She was a real victim that had not perpetrated any of these crimes upon herself. Yet, she couldn't help thinking that the whole world was looking at her disgrace. This kept her pain and dishonor fresh in her mind.

She believed that this meant her secret scars appeared on the outside too. She was convinced that everyone knew about her nights with strangers. She would play their imaginary insults over and over in her mind. She was beyond the feeling of humiliation and shame.

Each day continued with the same timeless routine. She would have been glad to welcome any sleep, but she was always treacherously betrayed. She hated turning in yet, she was so exhausted at the end of the day.

She had the kind of dreams that would make her lock up and sit silently, waiting to die. In these dreams there was never any escape. It seemed almost impossible for her to wake up without being sick and afraid. If it was not one of her captors, then it would be one of her brothers or sisters screaming for help. The images were always the same.

When she did awaken it was not without ice cold sweats. Her body and her clothes were drenched and she would shake and tremble with fear. It would take her literally hours to regain any composure because the memories that clung to her consciousness were so fresh.

There seemed to be no difference between day and night there in her mind. The images of ISIS invading her village would invade her reasoning without permission, and fill her with such dread that she only wanted to be buried with her father.

The sun, moon and stars were not indicators of a new day, or a moment that would pass away into some safe abyss. There was no escape. She was sure death would bring peace. She would experience at least one, and many times many of the random abusers infiltrating her dreams as she tried to doze off to sleep.

Time seemed to stop, but she was in a hurry to leave all of her horrid memories behind. She didn't feel any comfort with people around her, or ironically being without them.

Nadja was making an effort to try to get accustomed to her new accommodations. She was not forced to reconcile with the atrocities of her beloved village, but she had nothing to lose by shaking hands with her uncertain future.

She was in a constant state of panic, fear and rage. Her life had been taken from her, but she was still breathing in now strange place. She had certainly hoped that all of this would change. The place she was brought to was new, but the shock of losing her old life was making her as weary as the confinement by her captors.

On one occasion, she had retreated to her room and needed to muster up the courage to sit at the bare window. She thought that it may be time to face some of her fears. She could swear that she saw ISIS militants with every passerby.

Still she had noticed and was pleased that the dismal rains had finally left, and the sunlight would be her only welcome visitor for several days. It had really made no big difference and her outlook continued to be bleak.

Nadja was grateful but still hesitant about leaving her room. She did not want to mingle with the other people in the clinic unless it was well warranted. She turned down nearly all of the invitations to go out on field trips, unless they were mandatory, but many of the others seemed eager to explore the new country and landscapes.

Perhaps a new place helped them to forget their ordeal for just a little while. Although the center kept any outside news away from the women who were brought there, Nadja had already been through, and had seen far too much.

Painful memories that would last her for a million life times. The hideous reruns playing in her mind and subconscious were still her news every minute and hour of her day. Still, Nadja could not bring herself to believe that any of the people caring for her could possibly know the horrors that each woman had been subjected to.

Nadja was always afraid and bound in invisible chains. She trusted no one, not even herself. She was in a new place, and cautious of everyone and everything. She was on guard and desperately wondered about her own day-to-day safety even in this place.

She had always been really exposed to her attackers in the middle of the night. This became the hardest part of each day. She dreaded laying down in the bed and many nights had slept in a chair ready to fight her imaginary attackers should they enter her space.

But, there was something different that Nadja was feeling on one particular morning. She would be cut wide open and forced to visit her pain in its entirety. She was usually awakened by the distressing memory of the smell of burning tires and dead corpses. She could still picture in her mind the corpses piled high of her people, and then the machines that opened up the earth making a pit for the bodies to be cast into.

Nadja had followed her instincts and stayed behind. Then she had the misfortune of seeing one of the worst scenarios unfold before her eyes. For one brief occasion as she had left her room. She had begun to venture out to see other parts of the facility, and yet, hadn't gotten up enough courage to venture out to the market.

It happened just that way on one of those days a group of other women were being taken to shop and investigate the delicacies of the stores that were only a bus ride away.

The day was a warm and a beautiful sunny day that invited all of them, the women and the staff to walk and enjoy the marketplace. On that particular occasion, several women were taken with their small lunches in hand, if they chose not to stop at an eatery, and given money to learn to shop again. This would be a part of their therapy which would aid them in their getting use to normal settings and activities again

She had to stand by and watch a woman being brought back to her room shaken, shattered, and so frail that she could not even walk on her own down the hall. Tears streamed down the woman's face. Each staff member fussed over her trying to get to respond to some kind of positive stimulus.

They were in Germany, but terror had even followed these women there. There was no getting away from the shocking repercussions of being victims of a war that had nothing to do with them personally, only religiously.

Angela Merkel, the Prime Minister of Germany, had allowed Syrian refugees to come by the thousands. The people entering Germany were mostly men who held themselves up to be "refugees". They had no passports, documents, or any other papers that could identify their origins. Many of the men were fresh from Raqqa, Syria which is an ISIS stronghold.

The German Government allowed them in, and told them to wait for a period of time and then they would be given work permits. They were only identified as refugees, and not recognized by their prior "activities". The numbers of these men streaming in were enormous because of the war in Syria and IRAQ. These male refugees, without wives or children, flooded into every major city in Germany.

The women were out on one of their first trips shopping trying to regain some sense of normalcy when it happened. A few women were even courageous enough to go and find a bakery as they missed the fresh breads of the mornings in their village.

They were just minutes before stopping and talking with the Kurdish translator about the types of breads that seemed similar to those that they had even baked. Even though it was one individual It was devastating to all of those involved. No one could even imagine being confronted directly with the dark shadows of their past.

Just when the women were turning the corner to buy some fresh bread, one woman unexpectedly met with everything hideous that she had previously experienced.

On that particular day, during their adventurous and peaceful shopping time at the marketplace, one of the women had turned the corner just in time to come face-to-face with hell itself. He was one of her past rapists from Raqqa. Of course, he did not even recognize her. There were so many women at "their disposal" that these women had all looked the same to these filthy predators.

There had been so many women that had satisfied his sick, ritualistic behavior, that he had not even remembered that these were precious lives and individual people. But, she remembered him vividly and this set off so many unimaginable triggers that the woman had gone into a state of shock.

They brought her back to the care facility in their arms. She was unable to walk for several days. Nadja could not imagine the pain and the anguish that this precious woman was now suffering, and yet it was like yesterday.

Time had definitely made no difference. Each day had become an emotional sink hole. This poor woman confronted with her filthy rapist opened up a new series of old wounds in which now she had no place in which to escape.

Coming face to face with the terror of her not so distant past, this woman had been faced with a heart-stopping episode that caused her and all of the other women to open up past and present wounds. This included Nadja, and she was not along on their outing, but the woman's cries only made things worse.

Each woman was there trying to find a way to cope, and make some small sense out of what the curses surrounding them had meant. "Why" was the word that plagued their hearts. The loss of life and purpose, and for what reason? The loss of all family and friends without any viable explanation. This made Nadja stop and think of what she would do do when faced with similar circumstances of seeing one of the monsters, and she had no idea.

Tragically, depression and the dread sense of moving beyond the recent past had become her close acquaintance. What had she done to deserve this pit? Why was she the one of many spared? She knew that answers would continue to elude her. She was so brutally mired in wounds and grief that she could not think to ponder any of these questions at that time in her shame filled, empty sub-existence. Nadja hated the throbbing ache in her heart that reminded her that she was now all alone.

Young Nadja tried desperately to take advantage of their good intentions by cooperating with each staff member since her arrival. However, every time they would seek to include her, ask her a general question, or invite her to join various groups who were assessing their own personal damage, she declined.

Nadja was feel totally overwhelmed. She would close down and just shutter with grief. She had concluded in her young mind that discussing the aftermath, that she was now faced with, was just as horrendous as the torture. They could not be separated or compartmentalized into tiny units of pain. The haunting memories were fresh, festering and shameful.

CHAPTER TWO

"THE YEZIDIS"

" We have to dare to be ourselves, however frightening or strange that self may prove to be."
May Sarton

Nadja was the oldest of the four children. She was considered to be a little leader in her household and in her school. Oral tradition was their way of life, and she had always been reminded by her family of their proud history in some way.

She loved hearing the stories and tried voraciously to sort out their meanings. The stories and traditions were ancient and no one could explain exactly from where or whom each tradition had been born. Nadja did not care as they gave her a sense of belonging and pride.

The Yezidis had always been in constant danger. Yet, Nadja played as a little girl feeling a sense of security. She loved her family, especially her brothers. Yousif was the oldest brother, and Walid was the youngest boy in the family. Nadja loved playing with Yousif's gorgeous black curls.

Walid's smile could light up an entire room, but he had a sweet yet naughty presence about him, that everyone really loved. He was unpredictable and he was afraid of absolutely nothing. He was the youngest boy, but so old for his years.

One time on the mountain while taking care of the sheep, he was confronted by a wolf. With a bit of quick thinking, he set a rag full of kerosene on fire, launched it at the aggressive animal, and sent the wolf running and howling away with his tail on fire.

He was intelligent, quick witted and brave, yet, Nasima, the youngest girl had constantly reminded Walid that she was his "big sister" and that he had better listen to her. He rarely did, however. Nasima was the youngest girl and she had a breath taking natural beauty about her.

She was so lovely with blonde curls and deep green eyes that spoke to a person without saying a word. She was quiet and pensive, living each moment, but she took enough time to wrap everyday memories into small precious packages for later.

She was passionate about learning and discovering. Nasima loved the animals as much as her brothers did, always talking to the little lambs newly born. Her Kurdish teachers even boasted about her as a gifted student. And, oh how she loved to write daily in her small diary.

However, mixed into every story, parable or stated tradition, ideas were constantly being reinforced that she or any other member of the Yezidi community, would be forbidden to socialize with anyone outside of their culture. Socializing on any level with any other outside culture always turned out to be a dangerous endeavor, and would never be permitted.

Cultures are just that: mirrors. Then there are the people who are in the business of trying to break the mirrors attempting to establish themselves as the "mirror masters" who allege that they are on some kind of imaginary higher plane than all others.

When in truth, they have just fallen in love with their own image. This can be through group thought, religions, factions, governments or all four. Yet, if people choose to exist together each group could see how one culture would complement the other, and not insist that others groups or factions become non existent.

Each man would gladly go to his death for his family, and that they did. Her mother and brothers and sisters were kept abreast of any changes that were noticed, especially where ISIS was concerned and they thought that they had a perfect escape plan well in place.

These plans failed and she now sat and thought about many questions, all without answers, and it now seemed like just yesterday that she was hearing the sound of her father's voice speaking to her two brothers who also, patiently tended the sheep.

He was always busy on his cell phone talking to the men in her community, listening to their concerns and then giving them the best answers he could in light of the circumstances. He was a brave and yet tender soul named Zidan. He would hug her sisters and her, but he was known as a forceful resistance fighter. He had relatives and colleagues daily seeking his knowledge, in the event there was going to be another imminent attack.

Not knowing what was ahead, this time in their history they would share their wealth, blood and bodies. This was their lot was it was forced upon them with tremendous pain and humiliation, all without measure.

She had learned that under the Ottoman rule in the 18th and 19th centuries alone, the Yezidis were subject to at least 74 known genocidal massacres, so the threats to their community were real, and that she and her community was in constant danger there being no exceptions.

They had counted the numerous bloody genocides against people by Islamic extremists and other invaders over the past millennium and a half: Assyrians, Babylonians, Medes, Persians, Arabians, Syrians, Southern Iraqis and others. They built their Temples high upon the mountain, rather than in the villages, in testimony to its greater safety, and they sought safety there when there were rumors of a possible invasion.

Smaller villages hugged tightly to the base of the mountain and all the way around it. Invaders could be seen from the ground, but by then it would be too late. Their original homes, with larger villages between four and nine kilometers from its base in all directions, were artificially created by Saddam Hussein to contain and control these villagers.

Yet, living close to the mountain meant that there was an ancient security system that held major risk to their survival. It compromised the need for farming in the flat Mesopotamian fields near the Euphrates River, against the need to be able to flee to the mountain whenever the next genocide occurred.

Living further away, as they did now, was risky for them, and this living situation favored attackers, but their return to their original villages was a slow ongoing process after the fall of Hussein. Their location assured only the survival of the core of the Yezidi people at the expense of many individual lives who farmed the fields if there would be any surprise attack.

The world did not care to embark upon finding out who these mysterious people held themselves up to be, and simply turned their heads. No one in the outside world really knew how to interpret the plight of the Yezidis, since they were so isolated into their own social and cultural institution.

There was no one on the entire planet to break their cultural code and understand their plight. Without enough guidance it was impossible to help them. So, all groups around the world turned their collective heads.

There were no human rights groups taking up their cause to exist. No Coca Cola commercials on their behalf. There was no UN funding to help them when they were starving and being murdered.

They were simply ignored because they were a people of mystery. This meant that they would be running for their lives at any moment. They had to contend with the whole idea that they were never going to be safe, and would probably never be left alone. No one including the elders particularly understood why, but were subject to this dark dilemma anyway.

Nadja thought about each day back to her beginnings. These pieces of information made her indisputably whom she characterized herself to be. The mountain is where she grew up breathing, knowing, and seeing no other way of life except that of her strong, resilient Yezidi heritage.

Her roots had run centuries deep and she was proud of her home and village. She was aware that if she were to continue living in the confines of the Yezidi normalcy, this is who she stood fast to remain. There had been so many significant events in her short 15 years in her village, but her life had not started out that way. She had grown up in a very happy and productive family.

Her father loved being a family man, shepherd, businessman, and soldier. But, he had especially taken time and taught her and her siblings the importance of nature. The natural environment of the Yezidis had kept what was left of this culture alive.

She loved the fresh mountain air and the sweet waters that flowed down the crevices of the mountain, readily available to quench their thirst and used to cook the family meals.

She loved picking delicious, fresh spices with her cousins along with bright wildflowers from among its rocks in the spring. There were ripe figs, olives, and pomegranates in the late summer, and favorite herbs in all seasons.

Their family sheep pastured on its sides and valleys, even along the rocky ridges, forming an endless grid of trails, fertilizing the soil as they were moved steadily across it by shepherds to prevent overgrazing. The mountain was both mother and father to them. It had been the salvation of the Yezidi people through thousands of years of invasions.

Nadja's world had been very limited. There was a beautiful but extremely small buffer from the eminent dangers that were discernible around every corner. Everyday was a filled a stupendous simplicity and the community had not wanted to be reminded of madmen and their conquests. The elegant but rugged Mount Sinjar was the primary refuge of her Yezidi people.

They had sought the caves for safety through the genocides wrought against them in past centuries. They drank year round from the cool water that flowed from its many springs.

The young people celebrated Yezidi holidays with picnics playing the the clear streams, wearing beautiful, bright colors as break the brown monotony of summer. They blended in with the bright red, purple, pink, and yellow wildflowers and rich green grass of spring.

The mountain was also a source of food for their bodies and souls. Old men with long white beards and flowing robes counseled them from the doors of its ornate limestone Temples.

Scholars cannot begin to agree as to the origins of the Yezidi's cultural and or religious beliefs. They go very far back and have many twists and turns. As far as anyone can tell, The Yezidi religion is made up of Christianity, Judaism and the Zoroster Religion or Zoroastrianism, which includes reincarnation. Yet, they believe in one god and are one of the oldest monotheistic groups or minorities in regard to their religious roots.

The Yezidis believe in a supreme being named Yasdan, whose seven great spirits include the Peacock Angel named Malek Tawwus. They believe that the head angel, Malek Tawwus, lost his way, but that he went back to God to apologize for his rebellion.

For the Yezidis, they contend that the devil is **not** responsible for anyone's actions, but each person has to take personal responsibility for their own life activities.

This specific belief has been with the Yezidis for centuries. Many religions have central ideas which blame most of their human shortcomings on Satan, but, with all due respect, each religion finds itself at a loss for defining good versus evil.

The sufferings and misunderstandings over the centuries have resulted in many misunderstandings and as the Yezidi People depicted as devil worshipers. They are far from this kind of worship, especially when they choose to ignore the concept of blame by trying to solve their own problems.

Yet, this has brought much pain and despair to this culture. Teaching children how to take life steps would then be required and some form of logical decision-making lies with each individual at the end of the day.

The Yezidis, who speak Kurmaji Kurdish, had lived peacefully in the Kurdistan Region for hundreds of years. They were different, they knew it, and wanted desperately to remain so. It was profoundly important to them to remain separate from the rest of the world.

They married only into their culture and cherished the idea of family. They loved their families and would do anything for them. They lived hard lives but never felt the sacrifice as they were still in the ease and comfort of their culture.

Whenever there was a huge disagreement or a discrepancy with the business community, there was always other brothers available to help the people sort out their problems. The Elders were paid and they all went on with their lives.

These Elders enjoyed their easy life and renumeration just being, somewhat available, and would, from time to time, even walk up down the streets of a village so that they would be the first ones to know of any existing problems.

The Yezidis practice a secret religion, but it is their religion none the less. The religion is believed to have been founded by Shaahid ibn Djarraah, the true son of Adam, and later restored by the caliph Yazîd ibn Mu'âwaiya (although there is no evidence that this latter individual was ever associated with the sect claimed by some to bear his name).

Another semilegendary figure revered by the Yezidis is the Sufi Sheikh ʿAdî ibn Musâfir (died c. 1162), who they believe was sent by the Peacock Angel to educate and guide the Yezidis. His tomb near Mosul in northern Iraq is the most important site of pilgrimage in the Yezidi religion.

First of all, their religion closely adheres to the Yezidi Black Book or what is referred to as *The Mishefa Reş* or the *Meshaf Resh*. It is one of two books on the Yezidi religion written in the style of a holy book in, again, the Kurmanji dialect of the Kurdish Language.

The *Black Book* claims to originate when the Lord descended Black Mountain. It is not divided into chapters and is longer than the *Book of Revelation*. But, most scholars agree that the *Book of Revelation* and the *Black Book*, which were published in 1911 and 1913, are 'forgeries' in the sense they were written by non-Yezidis in response to Western travelers' and scholars' interest in the Yezidi religion.

The first half of it contains a creation myth, beginning with the creation of a white pearl and Melek Taus the Peacock Angel, who is commonly known as Satan or the Devil. Then, here follows an account of the Fall of Man in which the forbidden edible plant is wheat. Bread is still considered a very deep subject in some way.

The other revered book for the Yezidis is the *Book of Revelation or Kitêba Cilwe*. It is claimed that the original text of the *Book of Revelation* is kept in the Yezidi village of Ba'idn and the original text of the *Black Book* is kept in the village of Qasr 'tzz at-Din.

However, they do reflect authentic Yezidi religious traditions that are still held very sacred to them. The actual core texts of the religion that exist today are the hymns known as *qwals*. Then this is followed by the names of ancient kings who belonged to the Yezidi community.

From the Black Book, The Yezidi culture has featured numerous bans related to speech, behavior and food. There are many verbal taboos, but the most universal of these is a ban on saying 'Shaitan (Satan)'. There is also the statement of food taboos of the Yezidis. These would include but are not limited to eating lettuce, pumpkin, fish, chicken, gazelle, or marrow.

Then there are personal and religious prohibitions connected with personal hygiene, one which is about water. The *Masxafe Resh* (Black Book) also discusses the creation of humanity, how the power of evil tempts one to disobey God's commands, and certain taboos against wearing the color blue, for one.

The discussion reverts to the information and lineage of the ancient Yezidi kings, and then the Book concludes with another account of the Creation, which is quite considerably different from the first.

Finally, they believe that the creation of Eve is after Adam has been driven from Paradise or the Garden of Eden. This is an inconsistent account from any other religious text.

Then there is also a mysterious mix into the Yezidi culture of Zoroastrianism. According to the teachings of Zoroaster, the supreme god, named Ahura Mazda, created twin spirits, one of which chose truth and light, the other untruth and darkness.

Later writings present a more dualistic cosmology in which the struggle is between Ahura Mazda (Ormazd) and the evil spirit Ahriman. The scriptures of Zoroastrianism are the Zend-Avesta. The language survives in isolated areas of Iran and in India, where its followers are known as Parsees. So, in essence they practice monotheism with the influence of other religions mixed in.

Finally in their scope and understanding of religion, Nadja's family, like other Yezidis, had strong feelings against Muslims, but they had few ill feelings about Christians. They believed that the angel Yazda made Jesus in the Virgin Mary at the request of God.

He had been taught that Jesus was the son of God, a prophet of God, and that Jesus was resurrected from the dead and will return in power to the earth one day. They believed that Taus prayed for Jesus when he was crucified, and soon after he was resurrected.

The affinity between Christians and Yezidis was historic, and Nadja sensed this, not knowing the specifics. Two apostles of Jesus, Thomas and Thaddeus, converted many of the Assyrians to Christianity in the first century A.D., changing their language to the Aramaic language that Jesus spoke, and exposing the neighboring Yezidis to that religion.

From the fifth century, monasteries and churches were built throughout the region. Islam invaded the region in the seventh century, bringing a string of genocides against the Yezidis, who, along with Assyrian Christians, stubbornly refused to convert to Islam even when it meant their certain death.

Christianity and Yezidism both began to decline from that time to the present in Northern Iraq. Protestant Christianity never established itself in Northern Iraq, despite ongoing attempts, until recent decades. Missionaries who came to the region in the nineteenth century were either killed for helping Christians more than Kurds or returned to the West.

Protestant American medical missionary Asahel Grant met the Baba Sheik (the hereditary spiritual leader of the Yezidis) of his day around 1840 near Mosul and was very well received with great hospitality.

He noted that the Yezidis practiced baptism, made the sign of the cross, took off their shoes and kissed the threshold in any Christian church, and spoke of wine as the blood of Christ, holding a cup of wine with two hands in respect.

Throughout their history the Yezidis have been subject to persecution by their Muslim and Christian neighbors. The Muslims do not regard the Yezidis as a "People of the Book," and some have even considered them to be a heretic Muslim sect.

This belief, along with their refusal to enter the military service, has at times been used by hostile governments to justify attempts at forced conversion and even extermination of the Yezidis.

Several horrible waves of religious persecution in the nineteenth and early twentieth centuries drove Yezidi populations into Transcaucasia. In general, the Yezidis have enjoyed more amicable relations with Christians than with Muslims (including Muslim Kurds).

Sinjar was the name of the District and the name of the Mountain that overlooked the Village of Singar. The village housed Christian groups that resided on one side of the village and the other side of the village contained the populous and mysterious Yezidis.

ISIS had their sights set on an invasion early on. It was here in Nineveh Province that the Islamic State was wanting to take control of this and surrounding territories. They had taken Ninevah and destroyed the ancient and priceless artifacts of that region. Each fragment was broken or sold to waiting buyers around the world.

"ISIS" as they are now referred to had declared a caliphate and were taking village after village. They were on a rampage of killing and raping as they moved through each sector leaving behind bodies and destruction.

One could argue that they came through the villages to capture the young girls and attempt to force religious conversion on the people, but as time went by, however, it was more about demographics and strategies then religion. ISIS wanted IRAQ and Syria at any and all costs.

The Kurdish and the Yezidis have had a complicated past, but the Kurds have usually offered their protection. This time, however, it was impossible. For centuries, the Yezidis have hid from threats in the mountains. That's why approximately 40,000 Yezidis fled to Mount Sinjar when the city of Sinjar was lost to ISIS. There would be an invasion like no other because they were deceived into believing that protection existed and that they were not being betrayed by Arabs in their village.

The Sinjar Mountains lie near the Syrian border, and because the way into Kurdistan from inside Iraq is blocked by Sunni militants, the Yezidis hoped to cross the mountains and make their way to Kurdistan through an alternative route. When Saddam was ousted in 2003, it first benefited minorities like the Yezidis. But, as al-Qaeda began to take control, the community was targeted. In 2007, coordinated bomb blasts in a village killed 800 Yezidis.

Ethnically Yezidis are often misidentified as Kurds just because they speak Kurdish. Yezidis, indeed, take offense at being referred to as "Kurds", but some scholars believe that they may indeed represent the remnants of the ancient Iraqi population.

Yezidis speak Kurmanji Kurdish and refuse to speak Arabic which has had them at a disadvantage when it comes to knowing what their enemies are conjuring up in their ongoing diabolical plans.

Mysteries can be costly. Many times causes people and groups to be misunderstood. In the Middle East, it is a liability when people stray from the adopted cultural norms. To be different from the existing groups is in and of itself is the liability.

Since their religion or fundamental beliefs have always been called into question, they have also been accused of not having one since they don't theologically comply with just one. There are always going to be variations to a theme in any religion. It is the one thing that never changes.

ISIS would only be satisfied with the total demise of this culture. Their idea of ethnic and religious cleansing was, in essence, was basically for this people to cease to exist. If there was a new religion introduced it would mean that every way of life that was common to the Yezidi People what have to be severed. Their lives and their culture depended heavily on what they had known as heir religious customs.

However, it would be through forced measures that ISIS would try to persuade this group of mountain dwellers to virtually upload a new foundational belief system. It would be impossible to demand a strong transition that was new to those who over the centuries have never shifted. Many have tried before ISIS and have failed to bring Yezedi tribes into a new way of religious thinking.

The Yezidis lived their lives to the fullest even though there were many health problems and other situations that rendered them almost helpless. Their only work was within their village. They were not allowed to work outside by order of the Iraqi Government. Still weekly there were weddings and celebrations.

Sometimes these would happened two or three times a week. When there was a death, the whole community would come together. They would honor that person for almost a month with food and speeches about that person's life.

Throughout the centuries, The Yezidians have never had one moment of rest. Groups have even argued from where they got their name. Some say "Yezidi" is a form or derivative of the Name of God. Others claim that is a Muslim or Islamic.

They were called "Yezidi, Yezidians, or Yezidisame" were references given to them when they were forced from Persia. It is something that no one really knows, and it matters only that they can be able to express to their children and their children's children their authentic origins.

The Yezidis liked it that way, and their only crime is that they desired to keep to themselves. There is no one who can enter their culture or religion. Only those born into the Yezidi community can belong to the religion; the Yezidis do not appear to accept converts. There are some people who want all people to be "the same", but Yezidis are already a people who are slightly mirrored by some other culture.

According to tradition, the Yezidis originated in Syria, near the area of Basra, and later migrated into the Sinjar region of Iraqi Kurdistan, where they adopted the Kurdish language. Some Kurdish scholars even hold that Yezidism was the national religion of the Kurds in the Middle Ages.

Almost all of the Yezidis speak Kurdish dialects similar to the Kurmanj dialect of most Soviet Kurds. The Kurdish language belongs to the Northwestern Subgroup of the Iranian Group of the Indo-European Family.

This was always a confusing postulated series of events for the Yezidis, however. They have always referred to them as Kurds, particularly at voting time, and surely he shared ancient bloodlines with them, but religion and culture separated them almost completely. This cast them to the lower position as a minority, somewhat protected by them yet also quietly despised.

The artificial attempts of the Kurds to assimilate the Yezidis into their own ethnic culture in the modern era was equally oppressive, if less violent, from what the Baathists of Saddam Hussein's regime had shortly before forced upon Yezidis, requiring them to register as Arab.

They were neither Arab nor Kurd, and just wanted both groups to leave them alone. Both Kurds and Arabs continued to attempt to control the Yezidi people in Sinjar District.

The Arabs claimed the Sinjar District to be under their control, but the Kurds, with their autonomous government in the northern Region composed Erbil, Suleimaniya, and Duhok Provinces, actually controlled it with their Peshmerga forces, making it a contested area. As a result, some schools were teaching in Arabic, while others were teaching in Kurdish.

Following the Gulf War in 1990-1991 and the enforcement by the Americans of a no-fly zone in Iraqi Kurdistan region, the Iraqi Kurds had autonomy. However, supply routes were blockaded by the Iraqis and the Kurds suffered great hardship.

This meant that the Yezidis had to strive to take care of themselves and their culture and religion were the other two distinct factors that still kept them autonomous.

The Kurds were not going to be allowed to remain on their own, as usual. The contempt played out through economic power struggles. Baghdad's Central Government paid the salaries of the teachers and administrators in the Arabic language schools, while Erbil's Kurdistan Regional Governorate paid the salaries in the Kurdish language schools. Land was registered in Baghdad rather than Erbil, as were births, marriages, and deaths, ration cards, and passports.

Nadja and her family lived in the small remote corner of the world that the bigotry of many Arabs and Kurds allowed. Some of them called her and her family "devil worshippers." This false concept had arisen from too many similarities observed between the devil of Hebrew, Christian, and Muslim scriptures and their own chief angel.

The Muslims had begun charging Yezidis with devil worship from the end of the sixteenth century. Nadja and her family worshipped God, who has many names, the most common of which is the Arabic Rabulalamin (Arabic for "God of all") or Khodey (Kurmanji for "God who creates Himself").

Most of the Yezidis were living in five distinct districts. There is the District of Sheihan, the most important, to the northeast of Mosul in northern Iraq. Then there is Jabal Sinjar, near the Syrian border, 100 kilometers due west of Mosul. There is Halitiyeh, in the province of Diyarbakïr (southeastern Turkey). Also, there lies Malliyah, to the west of the Euphrates, including Aleppo. Also, possession of land was confined in an area there is Sarahdar, the Yezidi settlements in the Caucasus region.

Subsequent to the rectification of the frontier between the USSR and Turkey in 1921, the Yezidis in the Surmaly District were resettled in villages near Mt. Aragats (northwest of Yerevan), which had been abandoned by Muslim Kurds and the Turkish.

This meant that the Yezidi's and Armenians were coexisting and were very glad to live with each other. Both groups had tried to fight or inherently run for their lives on a frequent basis.

Many had relatives in Armenia and Georgia. They had ran to Russia in previous years and finally settled in these two areas. The largest waves of migration were subsequent to the Russo-Turkish conflicts of 1853-1856, 1877-1878, and 1914-1918. Some of these Yezidi newcomers settled in Armenia; a smaller proportion of them continued on into Georgia. By 1916 nearly 5,000 Yezidis were living in Tbilisi, the Georgian capital.

The Yezidis still had a relatively good reputation within Armenia, and many sought to one day travel to this land and investigate their lost ties with distant relatives there. Some were discouraged though, because in urban areas, their socioeconomic status was a bit lower than that of Armenians, although assimilated Yezidis are accepted as the equals of members of the majority population. They did not desire to lower their standards when they were doing just fine in the Province of Sinjar.

The social world of rural Yezidis is somewhat separate from their Armenian neighbors, however, because of the strict Yezidi caste system. Yet, in general, the economic role of the Yezidis is very well respected, and there is no interethnic conflict or hostility which is highly important. Business is business. This plays out purely to great economic means and ends for both populations.

So, it is no wonder that particularly close ties have been established and evolved between the Yezidis and the Armenians. These are their fellow sufferers in many persecutions within Ottoman Territory. The Armenians have also, been threatened by genocide and the most recent occurrence was in 1915-1917.

It was at this time that over 1.5 million Armenians were slaughtered. By the 1830s, many Yezidi tribespeople were being allowed to settle in the province of Yerevan. This would be a place that would help the Yezidi people stabilize until the next attack. For example, The 1877 census counted 8,000 Yezidis in the province of Yerevan, and over twice that many were recorded in 1912.

The Yezidis also had become very friendly with Christians who did not try to convert them, particularly if they could derive some natural benefit from them. They preferred to live with them rather than to live amongst Muslims. There was no sense that the Christians were trying to harm them, and were even generous to them in times of need, but they imagined that the local Christians looked down upon them. This was mainly because of the differences in personal cleansing and hygiene practices.

Indigenous Christians did not try to convert Muslims in Iraq as it was against the law and could result in their incarceration. A single incident could cut off the Muslim government's funding of their churches and communities whether in the period of Arab domination of Yezidis or in the more recent era of Kurdish domination.

There was no law against converting Yezidis to Islam, Christianity, or other religions, but the leaders of the Yezidis could put pressure on any organization involved in such activities to have their residency cards revoked and their organizational license cancelled. They could also try a person or an organization in the court of public opinion, if not in a court of law for proselytizing

Each group held a deep respect for the other even though they had some major differences in religion and culture. The Yezidis had to fight back to avoid total elimination, the Yezidis felt forced to defend both themselves and the Christians against the Ottomans in 1915-16, giving the Armenian Christians shelter on Mount Sinjar.

So, this mountain was considered sacred and a safe place for many decades. During the nineteenth and early twentieth century ethnic cleansing of Yezidis, many Yezidis fled to Christian areas of Georgia and Armenia. In the second half of the twentieth century, many of Turkey's Yezidis, emigrated to Germany, a predominantly Christian country.

In the second half of the twentieth century, many of Turkey's Yezidis, emigrated to Germany, a predominantly Christian country. Then there is the whole religious culture.

There was no facility for conversion from other religions to the Yezidi religion, because they believed Yezidis are repeatedly reincarnated only into faithful Yezidi adherents or animals, so ideology had never driven them to violence the way it drove extremist Muslims to conquer other cultures on their borders.

If the spirit had been bad in the body, it would go to the fire for punishment, and could only be reincarnated as a donkey or a disabled person or someone with a large birthmark, rising to higher status only through improved living and subsequent reincarnation. If the spirit was good in life, it would be reincarnated into a healthy baby from faithful Yezidi parents or go to heaven.

Through successive reincarnations, Yezidis thought that they could attain greater spiritual purity, and ultimately, divinity (which they believed Sheik Adi achieved in the twelfth century). They could not go to heaven unless they wore a white Yezidi undershirt and lived a pure life.

But reincarnation had no practical spiritual significance to them, unless they were a reincarnated angel, as they had no former memory of their former lives in other bodies and no powers derived from being reincarnated from a non-angelic being.

Any Yezidi who converted to another religion was rejected from the Yezidi culture, and could not be reincarnated upon death into a healthy Yezidi body.

A further similarity between the devil and Taus centered on the angel's rebellion. In Yezidi tradition, God told the angels to worship none but Him, so when he later made Adam, and told Taus to respect man, Taus rebelled as it seemed inconsistent with God's previous instruction.

He complained that man was made of dirt, and not worthy of worship. God cast Taus into the fire because of this rebellion, where he spent 40,000 years weeping. His tears put out the flames of hell and demonstrated his repentance, so God restored him, praising him for having tried to worship God in good conscience despite his mistake.

This story was seen as similar to the mention in Christian scriptures of the rebellion by the devil and his angels against God, and the resulting war between those angels and the angels of Michael who were faithful to God.

The difference, however, was that Taus was eventually praised by God, in Yezidi tradition, for trying to obey Him in good conscience though confused by seemingly conflicting requests.

In other traditions, the devil remains opposed and rejected by God through to the end of human existence on earth. The imposing stone relief of a big black snake on the wall at the entrance to two of their primary Temples, Sheik Adi Temple in Lalish in the Kurdistan Region, and Shekmand Temple near Jedali on Mount Sinjar, fed into the misconception of Yezidis as devil worshipers to those who believe Satan took the shape of a snake to tempt the first woman, Eve.

The snake was meant to symbolically guard the Temples from intruders the way lions guard shrines in Israel or eagles guard government buildings in the U.S. or gargoyles guard buildings of all types from the Europe of 150 years ago.

Their presence did not imply worship of animals any more than their prayers toward the sun in mornings and evenings constituted sun worship. The ancient Sufi Muslim leader Sheik Adi who had come to the Yezidis in the twelfth century, changing both their beliefs and his, had a real black snake that he left to guard the Temple in his absence, and the symbol was meant as an honor to that respected former leader. He died in 1162 and was buried in the Lalish Temple.

Living so far from modern civilization in a somewhat reclusive culture, their standards of personal cleanliness were more closely matched to those of others in the region, and people who lived in the rural areas of the U.S., Europe, or other western countries 150 years before, prior to the days when the public widely embraced the germ theory of disease.

The majority of people within every ethnic group in Iraq calls all other groups "dirty," which is an expression used more to define lines of intimate social acceptance and intermarriage than a careful assessment of physical cleanliness.

If food was served on platters on the floor or carpet, and the bread was laid in the floor where people had just walked, near the platters, it might be lifted off the floor and placed directly on the food for consumption in some homes. Relative cleanliness varied widely between families of course, and those with more education were generally cleaner in handling food.

Yezidis had also been called "dirty" simply because they didn't bathe on Wednesdays. This was important as a ritual purification of the soul similar to fasting, commemorating the visitation to earth of the chief angel, Taus. The first Wednesday of April each year, was marked as their New Year's Day.

The truth of this custom had been stretched through bigotry to say that he, and all Yezidis, rarely bathed. It was true that they ate over a cloth on the floor, with their hands, and they were very poor, so they couldn't always afford certain luxuries of cleanliness, but their homes were generally very clean, and the people generally bathed at least every three days, some every day except Wednesday.

Nadja followed strict local Yezidi customs without knowing the reason for any of them. She and her family didn't eat broccoli, lettuce or cabbage. They didn't wear clothes that may have been worn by Muslims. They, also would not allow Muslims to sew the neckline of her dresses worn by the women in her family.

Muslim extremists slitting the throats of their ancestors was given as a reason they didn't want Muslims making the necklines of their dresses. No one was allowed to wear v-neck tops. Others said it was a commemoration to the light God put around the neck of Taus.

The list went on and on for traditions practiced throughout modern history in Yezidi Culture. But, these were not necessarily the reasons for these historic traditions. They didn't wear the color blue, and the boys always wore two shirts, with the undershirt made in their home, the outer shirt purchased from the markets.

Someone had told Nadja that Muslim invaders once put blue flags on the houses of Yezidis they had conquered, and this is why they didn't wear blue.

Her father and brothers dressed while standing up, and she found out from her brothers that the men didn't urinate while standing, as expressions of respect for the name of God and his angels.

They didn't kill swallows with their black wings and white breasts because they resembled their black-robed holy men. On their New Year's Day, which was Wednesday in the first week in April, every family was required to have meat.

The wealthy, a lamb or an ox, the poor, a chicken or something else. They were to be cooked the evening before, and blessed at sunrise. They would then after eating the meat, take small portions of the food which were to be placed on tombs in the cemetery, where women would sing lamentations.

This was followed with picnics in the mountains by the people of every village. The girls gathered red flowers from the fields, tied them into bouquets, and after three days hung them on the doors as a sign that all people in the house were baptized Yezidis.

The water for their baptisms and ritual washings after traveling distances was to contain sumac and oil. One room under Lalish Temple was filled with jars of oil brought by people for the rituals.

Anti-Muslim sentiment was strong in Nadja and her family as in most Yezidis. She had been told that Mohammed had been enlightened by God, though the oppression Yezidis had experienced from Muslims continued to threaten their existence.

Nadja believed the Kurds had broken off from Yezidis when they embraced Islam. The Muslims said the opposite, claiming that Yezidis broke off from Islam, so they were heretics worthy of death.

The Muslims also counted Yezidis as "not people of the book," though Christians and Jews were given higher status by Mohammed so long as they did not threaten Muslims. Yezidis believed Islam would be defeated when Jesus and the angel Taus returned to the earth, "very soon." Muslims and Yezidis kept distance between themselves, preferring to live in separate communities.

Friendships did sometimes form between them, however, on a personal level, that overcame some of the bigotry. Normally the pleasantries did not extend beyond sharing tea or making simple business transactions, and there was no quick solution to these arguments as both religions or groups stood their dogged position.

Nadja was young but she was extremely aware of her community's efforts to survive the hatred and the constant threats that was always hanging over the heads of the Yezidis. She also, knew what was expected by each Yezidi, especially the women.

The peaceful village of Sinjar was seeing more and more violence escalate as a result of religious differences. The Yezidis began to flow back to Jedali and other small villages slowly after Saddam Hussein was removed by the joint efforts of American and Iraqi forces.

With Shia Muslims sent in to control Mosul, Yezidis grew only slightly more comfortable going to and from Mosul for work, commerce, and education. The relative peace would not last long. Sinjar was a cultural experiment in Kurdistan not a place for anyone to rest.

The Province of Sinjar is one of natural and etherial beauty. This was an exquisitely simple place with land that loved and nurtured the souls of the Yezidi People.

Everything that God could supply to take care of people was remarkably right there in the mountains. Timeless beauty with flowers that tinted the landscape in spring, breathtaking sunrises and sunsets, mountains and the summer breezes.

There was real pure water trickling from the mountain streams. The short summer wheat, light brown in fully ripened head, waved effortlessly in the slight mountain breezes. This wheat, like them, was rooted in the ages-old Mesopotamian soil, unmoved.

Their bodies were made of this soil, nurtured by what it produced, and they believed that one day they would lie beneath it, becoming one again with the countless others there: Yezidis, Kurds, Assyrians, Babylonians, Medes, Persians, Israelis, Greeks, Monguls, Turks, Syrians, and others.

Those under its soil had been born there, had sought out this land as a refuge, were forced onto it, or fell there in wars over power, glory, riches and ideology. The only question left for Nadja's family was when and how they would join them, in ripeness of age, in violent battle, by accident, or by disease, and how they would live their life before their eternal rest? It was a historic land.

They inherently believed that Noah floated across it in his ark and his children established its first cities along the Euphrates and Tigris rivers: Nimrod, Erech, Akkad, Calneh, Nineveh, Resen, Rehoboth-Ir and Calah. The Father of Faith, Abraham (who lived from about 1813 to 1634 B.C.) travelled through it on his way from Ur, south of Babylon near the Persian Gulf, to Canaan.

The Hebrew prophet Jonah preached in this area about the eighth century B.C. Jonah died in this area and his tomb in Mosul was blown up by ISIS on July 14, 2014.

The Hebrew prophet Nahum preached there a century later before the city was destroyed. Nahum's tomb is still intact to this day, in the nearby Christian village of Alkosh (Arabized from the original name El Kosh).

This was an ancient land that had held the Israelis who were captured and taken to Babylon. The Southern Kingdom of Israel was conquered by Nebuchadnezzar and its 20,000 captives travelled in the sorrow of defeat through the region on their way to exile in Babylon between 587 and 591 B.C., including Ezekiel, Ezra, Daniel, Shadrach, Meshach and Abednego.

But in another reality, Kurdistan is a land-locked country dependent on its neighbors for access to markets for both supplies and to export oil – Kurdistan's main economic resource. Turkey and Kurdistan are neighbors that are equally dependent on each other. The Region of Kurdistan spans four countries, Syria, Turkey, IRAQ and Iran.

Given the history of the region and the geographic significance of Kurdistan as one of the crossroads of the Middle East, the potential for continued conflict is extremely high.

Kurdistan has high hopes to survive as an independent nation-state one day, but it must prove to be strong enough to defend itself against the inevitable existential threats that will present itself and establish peaceful relationships with its neighbors despite a history of conflict, distrust and grievances. ISIS is still one of the main threats.

ISIS had designs on Sinjar for their own military purposes, however. Again, within Kurdistan is Sinjar. The group called ISIS had already conquered Nineveh Province.

With that, the Islamic State was determined to take control of this and surrounding territories. They had declared a caliphate and were taking village after village. They were on a rampage of killing and raping as they moved through each sector leaving behind bodies and destruction.

One could argue that they came through the villages to capture the young girls can attempt to force religious conversion on the people, but as time went by, however, it was more about demographics and strategies then religion.

ISIS wanted IRAQ and Syria at any and all costs. Sinjar is important to ISIS because of Highway 47, which lies alongside the town and links the Islamic State group's two biggest strongholds — Raqqa in Syria and Mosul in northern Iraq. The 120 kilometer (75 mile) -long highway has been one of the most active supply lines for ISIS, a major conduit for goods, weapons and fighters.

In October 2004, Ansar al-Sunna, a Sunni Muslim group in central Iraq opposed to the U.S. presence in Iraq and U.S. support for Israel released a video beheading of a Turkish truck driver on its website.

The group was formed by Abu Musab Al-Zawakiri, a militant Palestinian Islamist from Jordan with an intense hatred of Israel. He had been raised in a poor mining town north of Amman and was a petty criminal as a youth. He had fought Russians in Afghanistan in the 1980s.

He returned home to Jordan and tried to overthrow the Jordanian government. Explosives were found in his home, and he was arrested, convicted, and imprisoned in 1998. He spread radical views against Jordan, Israel, and the U.S. in prison, and controlled other prisoners for his purposes. A general amnesty in Jordan saw his release in 1999.

The next year, he was sought by the Jordanian government for trying to blow up the Radisson Hotel in Amman before New Year's Day 2000. He fled to Pakistan, but was deported to Afghanistan, where he affiliated with Osama bin Laden's Al Qaeda, receiving $200,000 in startup funds from bin Laden, and started a training camp for targeting American soldiers with chemical weapons.

He was wounded by U.S. soldiers in Afghanistan, and sought medical treatment in Baghdad, then moved to Syria to begin training fighters to resist the Americans. On October 28, 2002 his group shot and killed Laurence Foley, Director of U.S.A.I.D. in Amman, Jordan. The Americans continued to seek his extradition from every country where he was seen, without success.

Beheading was the manner of violence made popular by Zawakiri that was extremely effective in producing terror. It was not common to Al Qaeda outside Iraq, which preferred impersonal bombings in densely populated areas, but was the unique signature of Zawakiri.

He was self-declared the "Emir of the land of the two rivers" and cultivated a following of disaffected Sunni Muslims in Syrian and Iraq between Raqqa and Mosul. He boldly declared: "In the Name of Allah, I will not leave Iraq until victory or martyrdom!"

It was the U.S. presence there as a target that attracted him, and their ongoing support for Israel. He preached the overthrow of the Jordanian government, Israel, and the U.S. government, which remained cornerstones of the plans of his followers..

He affiliated with the Mujahideen Shuria Council in Iraq, which also affiliated with bin Laden. In September 2005, the Iraqi government's Shia forces attacked his militants in Tel Afar.

As a result, Zawakiri declared war on Americans and Shias everywhere in Iraq. He sent out suicide bombers to American and Shia Iraqi military posts. In revenge, a United States Air Force F-16C jet dropped two 500- pound (230 kg) guided bombs on his safehouse in Baqubah on June 7, 2006, killing Zawakiri, one or more of his wives, one of his sons, and some of his associates.

But his style of killing and use of the internet in brief video segments of beheadings, particularly of westerners, was adopted by his followers and continued in the area between Mosul and Raqqa. Osama bin Laden bristled at his rapid growth in power, his independent decision-making, and the media attention he received, so the relations between them were strained.

Also, his group adopted the historic hatred of Sunni Muslims toward Yezidis in the Iraq-Syria border area. They hated them for not being "people of the book" and for their stubborn refusal to "return" to Islam from their heretical beliefs. The return would be impossible when they had never embraced Islam from their very beginnings.

Again, as different leaders took power, so did the leaders of the Yezidi community. The Yezidis were also adamant about their culture and belief systems and refused to even give ear to any outside group regarding their religious beliefs and if they did or did not have "a Book".

They warned their young people about "mixing" over and over again. Although, the various communities share neighborhoods, their children attended schools together, and the groups had to come together to discuss politics, there was no ethnic crossing over permitted.

This was demonstrated in the most monstrous way. Public executions made it clear that those who headed up the Yezidi community would not permit any outsiders to desecrate their blood lines.

The world saw what rage festered between the two groups when the Yezidi's publicly punished a young girl who is now an international symbol remembered through the acts of barbarism that took her life.

The incident on or about April 7, 2007, totally shocked the entire world. The horrible occurrence was filmed in its entirety, and placed on YouTube as a blood-thirsty mob of about 2,000 men wanted death and no less for her.

Du'a Khalil Aswad, was a 17-year-old Yezidi girl who lived in Bashika, in the Nineveh province area between Mosul and Erbil. It was one of the few small towns in Iraq where Muslims, Christians and Yezidis lived together.

She fell in love with a Sunni Muslim boy from her neighborhood. The two had stayed out talking after dark one evening in their neighborhood, and they were both seen by her father and uncle. Terror struck their hearts as this was forbidden.

So, fearing for their lives, they sought refuge in the local police station, but the police would not get involved and handed them over to a local Yezidi Sheik.

The phones in the village were on fire with calls about the behavior of this girl and how she should be punished. They would not relinquish their charges, and her family members were pressured to move against her.

They claimed that she had converted to Islam, possibly married a young Muslim boy, and had run away with him. There was absolutely no proof of a sexual relationship between them, or that they had even tried to run away.

They were only talking privately in the open air in their own neighborhood. Her family was consulted by telephone, and the sheik convinced her that she had been forgiven of the dishonor she had brought to them, and could return home to her family.

Unknowingly to their dismay, the strange rumors were now being considered as "pure" fact. The young couple left the area to go to their respective homes. They began to go their separate ways, feeling the worst of the danger was now passed.

However, when Du'a started to walk toward her home, a mob of her relatives and other Yezidis met and accosted her. She was afraid as they insulted her, but then they placed her in a headlock and dragged her into the town square. They then pushed her to the ground.

She was stripped her of her clothes to shame her, and they continued insulting her for having insulted their religion and her family by talking to a Muslim boy without a male family member present. For thirty minutes they insulted and taunted her, while she begged for help from the ground, bloodied and bruised.

Their frenzied behavior escalated when someone threw a stone at her, and others followed suit, as was common among Yezidis in such cases. They began to stone Du'a to death. The final blow was made using a huge piece of concrete block that was used to crush her skull.

When the video of the incident, taken on a cell phone, was posted to the internet, it showed the police standing by idly. Her body was dragged through the streets by rope behind a car. They killed a dog and buried her with that same dog to further shame her.

Later her body was exhumed in an attempt to determine whether or not she had been a virgin. The information from the results were not circulated. Had she not been a virgin, the results certainly would have been circulated by the community as evidence in their favor as the international outcry grew and reporters descended on the town.

This violence by Yezidi men toward young Yezidi girls was as wrenching, horrific, and unjustified as any violence the Muslims had ever wrought against the Yezidis. It remained hidden to a large degree, tolerated by appointed government authorities in Yezidi communities.

For a brief moment it shocked the world, then people forgot about it and went back to their lives, as if it was a single newsworthy event. It was not a single event. Hundreds of Yezidi girls and women were stoned to death in Iraq, or burned to death, or burned themselves to death in the years before.

The evidence was available, in photos of hundreds of victims compiled into a thick album in the back room of one of the few Yezidi organizations in the Nineveh plains area.

Stoning deaths had been occurring in Tel Azer for centuries, but information about such events rarely reached the public outside the Sinjar area. When asked about such events, Yezidis said the girls who had been killed were bad for all the people.

Boys were rarely the victims of stoning. The exclusive reason for stoning deaths was love interest between Yezidis girls or women and Muslims boys or men, and sometimes sexual activity outside of marriage. The women always claimed to be innocent, and their claims were never believed. They had no concept of rape.

In every case, the woman was stoned to death, banished, or made so miserable she burned herself to death. The man was sometimes killed, if he was Muslim, and other times merely banished, particularly if he was Yezidi. Sometimes the Yezidi man was banished by the family, and sometimes he was also banished from the Yezidi religion by regional religious leaders.

These were the equivalent of lynchings, lacking any court involvement or summary decision-making by anyone other than that of the families involved or local Yezidi police acting as judge, jury, and executioner.

If the accused had any minor charge that could be proven in the slightest manner a group came together, and this ultimately resulted in a mob murder. Even the muqtars or elders were not usually involved.

CHAPTER THREE

"THE INVASION OF SINJAR"

" For what is evil but good tortured by its own hunger and thirst."
Kahlil Gibran

Things had been escalating in Nadja's village for a long time. With each tragic event tempers were flaring. The Muslims were feeling insulted as Yezidi boys and girls were being killed for even talking to other Muslim teens. Things were out of control and each group of elders would not budge one inch on what they considered their moral, religious and cultural ground. No one would be willing to back down on what they had held dear for centuries.

The younger people, however, were craving some kind of cultural reform, since they were going to school together, had grown up in the same neighborhood, and lived near each other but on separate blocks.

In one usual scenario, the father of the girl agreed that she was guilty, agreed with her stoning, and called for the banishment of the boy, under great pressure from the community who had considered any limited evidence and called for her immediate stoning.

In 2007, a man in his 60's saw a man in his later 20's wearing blue clothes and standing with a Yezidi girl of about 17 in his neighborhood in Tel Azer. This was Nadja's neighborhood and she knew that things were about to escalate.

He knew the young man was not Yezidi because he was wearing blue clothes. The older man called her father, who picked up his handgun, loaded it, and went with the older man to confront the couple. They asked his religion, and he said he was a Sunni Muslim. They asked why the couple had been talking there. They admitted they were going to run away and marry that day, because they loved each other.

Her father, hearing his daughter say she loved the Muslim, pulled out his handgun and shot the man in his stomach. The man fell to the ground, screaming. The girl started crying and holding onto her boyfriend. The police arrived five minutes later. The story was told to the Yezidi policemen. They agreed that the man deserved being shot.

By then 50 or more men and boys, even small boys, gathered around, while the women on rooftops watching the scene. Then, with police approval, the father shouted "Hola Shekhadia" entoning the name of their famous Sufi teacher of the twelfth century, calling all the village to participate in what would be an execution.

Yezidis within earshot to attack and kill the couple. All the people started throwing rocks at the man and killed him. The police took his body away. The girl was taken home by her father. Three months later she poured kerosene on herself and burned herself to death in a storage room in their home.

In 2013, a young Yezidi woman of about seventeen in Tel Azer fell in love with a Muslim boy from Sinjar city who came to work as a laborer framing the concrete roof for a new addition to her house. The boy came to the checkpoint in his car to wait for her. He was questioned at the checkpoint by volunteer Yezidi guards, and told them he was waiting for a girl to come to meet him so they could run away.

He actually declared his love for her and was determined that they were to be married. This sparked another incident and the Yezidi Community was up in arms. He was not going to abandon his love for her and the guards acted quickly.

They proceeded to check his ID and found out that he was a indeed Muslim. They grabbed him, tied his hands behind his back, and called her family, telling them about the situation, and asking them to come to the checkpoint. The family of the girl arrived, and immediately started throwing rocks at his car, severely damaging it.

The police were called, and came to take the boy to jail. He was arraigned in court and released. The family returned home with their daughter. The father told his daughter he was going to kill her for dishonoring their family and their religion by trying to run away with a Muslim.

The mother had taken a softer stance, and helped her run away to Zakho. She settled there, and married a Yezidi boy from Zakho, remaining estranged from her family. Burning suicides were also common due to the oppression of young women.

In a Sunni home, a 27-year-old unmarried woman, the only daughter in the family of five boys, was living with her parents. Her father and brothers were getting drunk regularly and fighting with her.

She often ran to her aunt's house next door crying, looking for an escape. She said she couldn't continue living there any longer, and didn't have a boyfriend to take her away. She told her aunt one day she would probably never see her again.

The next day, inside her kitchen, she poured kerosene on herself and lit herself on fire, suffering horrible burns. She was taken to an emergency hospital two hours away in Duhok for treatment, but she died there three days later. The family buried her and had a funeral dinner in her honor. Her mother was devastated, and added the loss of her daughter to her own continued suffering.

The terrorists were angry that Du'a had been killed for loving a Muslim boy. It pushed a red button for them that people in the west might not understand. Their response was a carefully planned and coordinated massacre of Yezidis.

On April 23, 2007, there were two reprisal attacks against the Yezidis, claimed by the Islamic State of Iraq. In Mosul, a bus filled with workers from a textile factory was pulled over on a lonely road. The attackers boarded the bus, and checked ID cards, which carry the religion designation in Iraq. Muslims and Christians were told to get off the bus.

The attackers drove the bus with the Yezidis on board to the eastern outskirts of Mosul, where all the hostages were forced to lie face down on the ground and shot dead. This exact style of killing was soon to resurface in attacks on Yezidis throughout the Sinjar District.

The same day a coordinated attack occurred in Teleskof. A car bomb detonated, killing the suicide bomber and 25 Yezidis and Assyrian Christians. The attack was claimed by Ansar Al-Sunna, Zawakiri's fighters. On August 14, 2007, Tel Azer and nearby Jazeera, two Yezidi villages, were bombed by large tractor trailers filled with explosives. In Tel Azer, 336 Yezidis were killed, and about 1,500 were wounded.

In Jazeera up to 300 more were killed, and an unknown number were wounded. This group continued to grow in strength, training in Syria, and preoccupied itself with struggles for land in Syria against President Bashar al Asaad. Meanwhile, its interest in Mosul and other parts of Iraq continued.

On May 16, 2010, the leader of the Mujahideen Shuria Council (MSC) was killed by U.S. forces at his safehouse near Tikrit. The council then elected Abu Bakir al-Baghdadi as its new leader. His actual name was Ibrahim Awad Ibrahim, born near Samarra, Iraq near Baghdad in 1971. He had been detained by the U.S. but was considered a low-level fighter. In detention, he rose to prominence by networking with the other terrorists of the MSC.

When Bin Laden was killed by the U.S. on May 2, 2011, Zawakiri vowed revenge. The fighters who had served Zawakiri joined forces with al Baghdadi, adding strength in the Mosul and Raqqa area, creating opportunities further north in Iraq and in Syria, and renaming their group Islamic State of Iraq (ISI) or later known as ISIS.

On May 2, 2011, the leadership of al Qaeda passed to bin Ladin's second in command, Egyptian surgeon Ayman Mohammed Rabie al-Zawahiri. He should not be confused with al-Zawakiri, the Iraqi terrorist, who was already dead at this point.

A conflict arose between al-Baghdadi and al-Zawahiri about the addition of fighters from Syria's al-Nusra Front into al-Qaeda, which resulted in the separation of ISIS from al-Qaeda, with about 80% of the Syrian fighters aligning with al-Baghdadi and ISIS.

This strengthened ISIS in Syria considerably, adding the new fighters to those inherited from Zawakiri. ISIS quickly began to use this influx of fighters to secure strongholds in the areas between Raqqa, Syria and Mosul, Iraq. On August 15, 2011, a wave of ISIS suicide attacks beginning in Mosul resulted in 70 deaths. It was clear by then that Mosul was their target.

Their successes there emboldened them. They were testing the defenses of Mosul, and found neither the Kurds nor the Arabs rose to its vigorous defense. They did not have to make any hard decisions.

They began developing plans for its overthrow. On April 8, 2013, al-Baghdadi announced that ISI had been reformed into Islamic State of Iraq and the Levant (ISIL), which was then altered to Islamic State of Iraq and Syria (ISIS).

Their increasing strength drew attention and funding from citizens in Saudi Arabia and Qatar, and brought fighters from Saudi Arabia, Morocco, Egypt, and other predominantly Sunni Muslim countries.

The people of Iraq referred to ISIS using its equivalent Arabic acronym, which, when read as a word in Arabic, sounded like "ISIS." ISIS leaders threatened to cut out the tongue of anyone calling them "ISIS" because that word in Arabic meant something close to "stamp out" or "destroy."

Since the term was coined as a word by their enemies, it conveyed a veiled threat to ISIS to stamp out their organization. That ISIS leaders took offense to their own chosen acronym when spoken as a word provided perverse pleasure to those targeted by the group. It was the only recognizable term for the group in Iraq.

The context was ripe for ISIS to reap huge temporary gains in the area at a low cost. Iraq remained deeply divided into two Muslim branches with long histories, over who was the rightful successor of Mohammed.

Kurds and Arabs both leveled claims to the Nineveh Plains area which included Mosul, but the Arab presence there restricted Kurds from making any moves, and the Sunni religion of its residents made the Shia government's control there weak.

Syria was weakened by opposition to the government and the interference of foreign nations that initiated bombing campaigns there. ISIS moved into the power vacuum and ruthlessly claimed lands that were the most vulnerable, making Raqqa their stronghold.

Mosul was particularly weak, and ripe for the taking. The U.S. government wanted democracy and majority rule to build peace and economic prosperity there. Their optimism that democracy would readily grow in Iraq despite deeply divided religious and geographical components was proven wrong.

The U.S. was unified along Christian principles when democracy developed there, so it was easy for the U.S. to miss the geographic/ethnic/religious divisions within Iraq as threats to democratic development.

The U.S. used simple math to see that Shia Muslims were in a majority over Sunni Muslims in Iraq, then replaced Sunni Iraqi leaders in Baghdad with Shia leaders, who quickly moved to dominate Sunnis in Mosul. The Shia had become cruel tyrants to the Sunnis, and had become despised in Mosul.

Unable to unseat their new Shia overlords alone, the leading Sunni men in Mosul allowed ISIS to enter in a bid to help them reclaim power over the city and the surrounding region. Then they joined ISIS as they entered to slaughter many and set others to flight.

A more fine-grained political calculus might have led the U.S. down a more fruitful path to democratic development in Iraq, but the U.S. remained poorly informed on the Iraqi situation.

It's agents in Iraq lived and moved in little security bubbles according to rules that kept them from gaining a deeper understanding of the forces at play, and broader public sentiments.

They met locals on their own turf, on their own terms, and were not good listeners. They hired people for their English skills rather than for their reasoning and reporting abilities.

On June 10, 2014, ISIS attacked Mosul and the nearby town of Tal Afar, parts of Kirkuk and Diyala Provinces, Tikrit and much of Nineveh Province in a sweeping victory.

Rockets had fallen on Christian and Yezidi villages to frighten the people, after which ISIS operatives made telephone calls to Yezidi and Christian leaders, ordering them to convert, pay a heavy tax, or evacuate.

A mass exodus of Yezidis and Christians from Nineveh Province had followed, to large cities in the Iraqi Kurdistan Region: Duhok, Erbil, and Suleimaniya. 1,700 Iraqi soldiers who had surrendered in the extremist Muslim attacks on moderate, chiefly Muslim, cities had been massacred.

ISIS was welcomed by the majority Sunni Muslims in Mosul and feared by the Shias who worked there as outsiders in a sea of Sunni discontent. For some very strange reason there were ISIS sympathizers.

When ISIS entered Mosul, the Shia overlords simply ran away for fear of retribution, while the smaller numbers of Sunnis in the Iraqi Army melted away in hopes ISIS would return power to Sunnis. ISIS went on to seize Fallujah, Al Qaim, Abu Ghraib, Ramadi and other cities and villages in Iraq that had once been "liberated" by U.S. forces.

With the conquered city of Tel Afar only an hour's drive from Nadja's home in Tel Azer, and with Mosul, a city of more than a million, growing into a center of operations for ISIS in Iraq not far away, all the people in his village were vigilant. Muslim extremism had been taking an even harsher turn than ever before in Mosul, and they knew they would eventually become targets.

Yet they clung to the hope they could escape to Mount Sinjar as they had always done in the past if they were invaded. They knew many would die if they were invaded but they could not afford to leave their villages, homes, and sources of income until the last moment of invasion. Their poverty gave them limited choices. Their separate peace in Tel Azer was threatened, and they knew it.

Peshmerga, which means, "those who face death," is the military of the Kurdistan Regional Government (KRG) and Iraqi Kurdistan. Their existence dates back to the mid-20th Century when Mustafa Barzani picked up arms to fight for Kurdistan autonomy. As the Kurdish nationalist movement grew, so too did the identity of the Peshmerga as a key part of Kurdish culture - evolving from tribal defenders to nationalist fighters for an independent Kurdish State.

The basic tradition of a guerrilla resistance forces fighting for Kurdish autonomy goes back to the origins of the Kurdish People. They are fighters that are familiar with the mountains and tough terrain.

The mountains have always been the friends to the Kurds and Yezidis. Because the land area has always been subject to regional and major powers vying for dominance, a resistance force always emerged as they took refuge in the mountains.

Up against much greater forces in the Iraqi Army and Air Force, the Peshmerga was not successful until after the 1990-1991 Gulf War when the U.S. and U.K. enforced a no-fly zone in the North of Iraq.

After the Kurdistan Regional Government was established, the Peshmerga officially became the armed forces and responsible for the security of the Kurdistan Region of Iraq.

The Kurdish and the Yezidis have had a complicated past, but the Kurds have usually offered their protection. This time, however, it was impossible. For centuries, the Yezidis have hid from threats in the mountains.

That's why approximately 40,000 Yezidis fled to Mount Sinjar when the city of Sinjar was lost to ISIS. When Saddam was ousted in 2003, it first benefited minorities like the Yezidis. But as al-Qaeda began to take control, the community was targeted.

In 2007, coordinated bomb blasts in a village killed 800 Yezidis. ISIS had also already captured many other Yezidi shrines. They were aiming their direct focus on the Yezidi Community in Sinjar.

They relied heavily on help from the Kurdish Peshmerga soldiers, though only about 40 were stationed there, but the Kurds also had the same old weapons the Yezidis had, and lacked adequate ammunition to defend the village from a sustained attack.

The village had no plan for evacuation. It would be every man, woman and child for himself or herself on a narrow road to the mountain passing near another village that might, itself, be under attack at the same time.

Dozens of Kurdish Peshmerga soldiers stayed closer to the checkpoint on the road. Most were from the northern portion of the autonomous Kurdistan Region of Iraq, speaking Badini Kurdish and loyal to the KDP party, and a smaller number were from the south, speaking Sorani Kurdish, loyal to the PUK party. These soldiers were on standby but were not engaging in battle in this region at all.

ISIS is attacking Kurdish cities in both Syria and Iraq. The Peshmerga is defending and attempting to retake cities which were previously under the control of the Kurds.

The Peshmerga, which also includes women, has shown to be an effective fighting force, but have few resources against what appears to be a well-financed and growing ISIS army.

America had sent in troops and supported Iraqi Kurdish autonomy and provided continuous direct military support in training and equipping Peshmerga as well as providing air strikes to destroy ISIS. Yet, the facts would prove that the problems had really begun to emerge years before.

Unfortunately, where the Yezidi People dwelt there within kilometers was the troops of The Islamic State of Iraq and Syria (ISIS), the latest existential threat, now controls a large swath of land straddling the Iraq and Syrian borders. Each group who was living in Kurdistan was protected without question, but for the Province of Sinjar it was not to be.

OUT OF TIME

That early morning before the raid, Nadja's two young brothers, Yousif and Walid were busy at work was tending their father's sheep near Jedali on the side of Mount Sinjar. The number of the sheep were about 350, and they were guided to safety for the night in a short enclosure adjacent to their father's garden. There was no food stored for the sheep.

They would be herded outside the edge of the village on the mountain for pasture. As they followed them out of the enclosure past the neighboring houses and along the unpaved village streets they would call to the sheep continuously, in their unique whistles, calls whoops, and that all the people and sheep understood fully. They were the most recognizable sounds around Mount Sinjar, a hymn of daily life with its own unique cadence and tones.

The boys rose early in the morning, like all mornings, to check on the sheep, and called to them with the reassurance each shepherd knew they loved. They immediately recognized the familiar voices that gave them safety, comfort food and water, and they would never follow any others.

The shepherds knew their moods, what moved them, what calmed them, their schedule, preferences, and habits. They were the mainstay of their family, their source of meat, milk, and yoghurt, wool for clothing and blankets, and hides to barter or sell in the market to get other needed items.

Their family had trusted their entire wealth to these two brothers, and their wellbeing of the rest of the children to them too. Final protection fell to their father, and the household to the mother and the girls. Also, in between, the boys took odd jobs outside the home to earn what they could, giving all their earned cash to the family. Each of them knew his place in this economy, and was faithful to it.

The sheep moved exactly by what to expect in their day to day routine, and they needed their shepherds to keep them from danger. They just had to be there with them for subtle cues to their movements upon the mountain.

Nature carried all the needed elements, oak trees to shade them, clean air, and abundant spring water to wash down the dry late summer grass. The birds that flew overhead or sang from treetops, and the eagles and sparrow hawks soaring on the updrafts near the mountain cliffs above, were ignored by the sheep but appreciated by the shepherds.

They walked out a distance from the sheep up the hillside, their eyes following the dusty rose-colored limestone rocks on the jagged crest of the mountain, following the line of its peaks and valleys accentuated by the shadows of the morning sun, an image painted on a canvas of limestone rock and dry grass. The ridge ran for over 35 miles over rough terrain.

At that early hour, a side of every rock, blade of dry grass, and green oak tree on the mountain captured the rising sunlight. There were long shadows cast from the eastern rising sun. On warm days there was not a drop of dew to vaporize or sparkle on the tall dry grass.

Everything seemed to move softly in the gentle breeze, because all was as dry as the brush that surrounded it. The mornings were glorious. The scorching sunlight of the afternoon would pierce the skin. Each one had to rush to the shade, but the pleasant light of morning that brightened and warmed the skin for a few pleasing moments, gave joy to the early morning routines.

But all that would change quickly. Little did the boys know that this would be the last day that they would tend their precious flock. They knew each sheep and had even named some after being born. ISIS was on the way and their sheep would be left to tend for themselves or they would be stolen and merged into another flock.

Trouble was always on the horizon for the Yezidis, but this time the darkness that would invade their village wold not compare with the 74 other attempts to commit genocide against this people.

There was no where to run or to hide. The Yezidi Community of Sinjar was out of time. Some of the people had already contacted relatives in different areas, but by August 2014, time had run out. On that particular morning, there were no Kurdish Military Forces in sight.

The Peshmerga, was mysteriously missing. They were always seen everywhere, but on that crucial morning there was an ominous disappearance of the military.

This was so surprising because during the weeks before the invasion everyone knew that things were at the critical point. The Yezidis did not speak of the horrors that could befall them, but chose to carry on with everyday life trying to project an image of calm.

Random gunfire even throughout the nights had set everyone on edge yet, no one chose to converse about it publicly. So many attempted genocides were in their past, but this one was different. The high powered weaponry coupled with radical extreme faction was a fatal combination.

The Peshmerga had been fighting the Islamist militants of their declared Islamic State - who had already seized large swathes of territory in the north.

Now thought to number around 190,000, the Peshmerga had their roots in groups of loosely organized tribal border guards in the late 1800s, but were formally organized as the national fighting force of the Kurdish people after the fall of the Ottoman Empire in the wake of World War One. This time they were ready but ill equipped. The boys would wave to them as they would pass by. They were always given a smile in return.

This would result in leaving the Yezidi Community totally helpless. There was not to be any help for the Yezidis or the Christians in the village. The Kurdish Peshmerga Forces had withdrawn from the area during the night. They were fighting with old weapons and had even run out of bullets. They many times had to buy their own because of having to confront these ISIS extremists in many areas.

ISIS was armed with state of the art weapons, and those being from the United States of America. With Hillary Clinton as Secretary of State and President Barack Obama not speaking out against the atrocities that were being committed by this terrorist organization, they were running through village after village seizing gold, valuables and the young Yezidi and Christian girls.

They then slaughtered the men and anyone who cared to get in their way. ISIS knew that the Iraqi troops had fled, and that he Peshmerga that protected Kurdistan, could and would not be able to help. It was also well known to them that Kurdistan, because of war was a region was already in deep economic distress.

The men were already talking about their Yezidi leaders, the most senior of which, Prince Tahseen, had already left for Europe for medical care in his advanced age, and was trying to block his people from following him into Germany.

They analyzed his motives for this action. He would be worried the people would likely lose their connection to their culture and religion, and that he and his son might see their hereditary rights to income and power weaken. They gently faulted him for leaving them without aid in the face of a looming invasion, then trying to block their escape to Europe.

He was the Yezidi leader that they had discussed irreverently and was supposed to be the liaison between the Kurdish government and their people, whom they ridiculed for dressing, acting, thinking, and talking more like a Badini Kurd than a Yezidi.

They ridiculed him even more for his personal financial benefit and not seeing to any of theirs. They discussed with more respect their hereditary spiritual leader Baba Sheik, some of the local elders who were fully woven into the fabric of their village, and a young woman named Vian Dakhil, who had become a heroine to them as their only representative in the Iraqi Parliament.

The concerned males were practical men, husbands and fathers, facing realities that would not go away, receiving little help from their leaders, other than Vian, who was in Baghdad doing what she could to help them. Salaam's father joined in with a laugh now and then and offered a nod to their more truthful remarks, but avoided speaking carelessly about dignitaries.

One of the men, Ismail Shammo Qassim was 48 years old. Just 52 days before, he had had a brush with ISIS, while he was on military duty with the Northern Brigade of the Iraqi Border Police, in Sunni on the north side of Mount Sinjar.

ISIS was approaching, though he didn't know it. Two hours before ISIS arrived, the representatives of Nouri al Maliki, President of Iraq, his superior officers in the Border Patrol, took away all the guns from his group of 20 Kurdish, Arabic, and Yezidi fighters.

They did not leave their post in Sunni even though they had been disarmed. No reason was given for disarming them. Two hours later, when ISIS arrived suddenly, and drove through without stopping, the policemen were still in the streets, with no time to escape and no arms to defend themselves.

One of the trucks rammed him, and he fell down on the ground, injuring his back and head. All of the men were able to escape before ISIS could capture them.

He shared his experience as evidence of the corruption of the President, adding that man to the list of other leaders who had been ill spoken of by the group of practical fighting men who had families to feed and support with little help from their leaders.

These discussions played throughout the night with cell phones ringing, but the callers were whispering. "They are here", was spoken softly. The ringing was keeping the men mentally alert, sharing essential information out the relative strength of various leaders upon whom they relied, allowing them to shape and reshape their working paradigm about the world in which they lived.

They were not a fearful people, but were interested in knowing what real threats were in play, so they would have some idea of how to counter them with their limited resources. They turned mostly at that point to their trusted Kalashikov rifles.

It was a hot day at the beginning of August. Nadja awoke to the sound of distant gunfire the middle of the night as she had done the night before. This was different. Her eyes flew open and she leapt to her feet, distinguishing between the single shot the night before and this lower constant drone of distant warfare.

It was 2:30 am. The sound, and abrupt movements going on in the house, startled her. Nadja looked out from the window and saw the red lights of mortars being fired on the two cities on either side of Tel Azer, Jazeera to the west, and Gazarik to the east.

Then she turned and looked at an old calendar that hung on the wall near the kitchen. The date was etched in her mind. It was August 3, 2014, and this is the day that ISIS fighters swept into the Sinjar region of northern Iraq, home to the majority of the world's Yezidis.

They rounded up the Yezidis into three groups: Young boys who were made to fight for IS, older males who were killed if they didn't convert to Islam, and women and girls sold into slavery.

Tens of thousands of Yezidis fled to the mountains, where the militants surrounded them in the scorching summer heat. The U.S., Iraq, Britain, France and Australia flew in water and other supplies, but many Yezidis died before they could be rescued.

Following the IS assault, "no free Yezidis remained in the Sinjar region," a United Nations expert panel wrote. "The 400,000-strong community had all been displaced, captured or killed." An estimated 3,200 are still in IS captivity in Syria, where they were taken after being captured. The attack by ISIS would be 3-pronged, effectively pinning the people of Tel Azer against the mountain, where ISIS hoped to capture or kill them.

ISIS approached Jazeera directly from Syria, entering from the west, with support from ISIS forces in Anbar Province seven hours' drive to the south and forces from Baaj, nearby to the southeast, with support from its Arab residents. Jazeera was the easiest target for ISIS, remote and small, and winning it fortified the terrorists to move toward Tel Azer directly to the East.

A similar attack was launched at the same time against Guzarik to the east of Tel Azer. Guzarik was attacked by ISIS forces from Mosul, supported by other fighters from Baaj and Anbar. ISIS fighters were assisted by Muslim Arabs from the surrounding villages bent on killing their Yezidi neighbors. The timing of this 3-pronged attack was closely coordinated to effect maximum human casualties specifically among Yezidis in this planned act of genocide.

Then, the worst scenario began to unfold and escalate right before Nadja's eyes. It played like a surreal horror movie. Her grandfather was shot because he refused to let go of his wife's hand. The savages would not allow any humanity to remain in the old man and as he fell to the ground, he still clutched her hand.

She screamed and they hit her so hard with the back of a rifle she was killed instantly. One killing after another in right there in peaceful Sinjar. Corpses were right on the road. These were the now lifeless men who had eaten and talked with her family since she could remember.

Nadja tried to calm her sister, Nasima, her brothers and even her whole family. "Mother we have to go to the mountain now and father will come later," Nadja offered, knowing that her mother Rooba was not going to accept that.

"Nawallah!" Rooba cried, Nasima and Yousif rushing to her side. "We cannot leave without him!" Zidan was a proud father and he was going to attempt to protect their family until the bitter end.

The two brothers had joined the three girls close to Rooba's side and now all of them were crying desperate tears. Nadja thought of her parent's helplessness, and longed to console them, but she would have to wait to see if conditions were going to improve. She could only hope. She phoned her father.

Her explanation of how serious things were, and the speed of the encroaching ISIS fighters, left no room for her father to argue with her on the telephone. Nadja's friend's brother and their cousins were Peshmerga, members of the Iraqi Kurdish military.

They desperately tried to inform every family, who would listen, that they couldn't fight anymore and that everyone should run away fast. Families should try and save themselves from ISIS. She knew that her family would wait for their father's instruction, but time was running out.

This, also, meant that all of them including any Peshmerga would have to evacuate their position sooner if it became clear that ISIS would breach the lines, or there would be no time to get the family to the mountain before ISIS swooped in with a wicked vengeance.

They had already entered the village. It was a careful calculus he had to work out in the midst of battle, and any slight error in timing could mean the end of his life and theirs. At 66 years of age, Zidan had to use his energy and time wisely.

As Nadja closed her phone, Rooba began to command the girls to gather the most important things for the journey to the mountain. But, packing in this climate meant there would be total confusion as what would be priority items. Going there before had always been for a picnic or a family reunion, but this would be something entirely different.

That upper part of the mountain had been a friend to their ancestors, in that it had saved a remnant of their bloodline from annihilation. The mountain was their friend so long as they rested in the arms of its gentle valleys of its lower reaches under fig, pomegranate, and olive trees by cool springs, but further up, the rocks were more forbidding, the water was less abundant, and food was scarce. There were snakes by day and wolves by nightfall.

Reaching there, and remaining there for any length of time, would mean certain death for many, and perhaps for them, as it had for so many before. Ultimately They would have to travel separately and meet at Qandil, an abandoned settlement that Saddam Hussein had bombed in years past that was now used for keeping sheep.

Nadja felt some relief as she had reached her father on the phone. She and their other family members were already preparing to go to the mountain, and knowing that set Rooba at ease. The fathers were being slaughtered and they had wanted to take so many neighbor children too, but the responsibilities were with and for Nadja's family now.

Their fate rested with that of Nadja's family, even though it put all of them at greater risk. She wanted to be with her family no matter where that was, no matter what the cost. The next five hours were tortuous for them all, knowing their father was fighting a strong force with limited ammunition.

Yousif and Walid had stationed themselves on the roof, watching the red lights from hot bullets and mortar rounds growing closer to the side where his father was stationed, hearing the sounds of gunfire and mortars growing louder. They could also see the people scurrying around the neighborhood, preparing to leave, and men grabbing their rifles and running to join the fight.

They could also see families being separated in the chaos, as people ran for their lives, screaming, shouting orders to children, and crying. The mass exodus gradually changed shape from the chaotic swarm within the village into a single line of evacuation on the road toward Jedali and the mountain beyond. It was composed of people, sheep, goats, donkeys, sheepdogs, and every kind of vehicle.

An hour after she had wanted to talk to her father again, growing more anxious, and unable to reach her father again by phone, Nadja called several neighbors to see if they knew anything of the other men fighting on the front line to assess the situation.

They all felt they could hold ISIS back. By the second hour, when Nadja called again, they had become less sure of themselves. There were about 200 Kurdish Peshmerga positioned to defend Tel Azer on the front line with rockets, rifles, and other weapons.

The Yezidi militia were there with them, men of every age, who volunteered for ten days at a time. For a while, they fought bravely and held ISIS at bay, but their ammunition was running low.

Then, it was not known to the Yezidis in the Province of Sinjar, that the final order finally came. The Kurdish Peshmerga received an order by telephone from their superiors at about 5 AM telling them to evacuate to the safety of Duhok. As they left, they promised the Yezidis they would send reinforcements stronger and better armed than them, so they should not leave their posts, but continue fighting.

They left one big gun for the Yezedis, but took the others away with them. The Yezidi men continued to fight. It was a mistake that would mean the deaths of many.

One of the Yezidi fighters, Ismail Shammo, fighting some distance from the Kurds, called a friend in the Peshmerga on his cell phone to find out what was going on, and the Peshmerga Soldier had said not to worry, they were fighting ISIS.

Later he found out that the Peshmerga had already fled but the soldier was apparently too ashamed to tell him. They could have reported their retreat orders to the muqtars, and may have, but the people didn't get the word.

Nadja called some of her other cousins who were Yezidi Peshmerga soldiers stationed in Solaq Village, and found that the Kurdish Peshmerga had totally abandoned the fight there at about 5 AM, and the Yezidi soldiers were now evacuating with their families, leaving no force to protect the village. She presumed the same was happening in Tel Azer, at about the same time.

Ibrahim Khudeda Baker, who was also fighting on the front line in Tel Azer, said: We called the Peshmerga to ask for help for our side of the line, and they said they would bring help in five minutes, but the help didn't come.

They fought until their bullets finished, and no one came to resupply us or help them. They called Sarbast (General Sarbast Baiperi, who was over Peshmerga for all Sinjar District) but he said he had retreated to the Kurdistan Region checkpoint, and they didn't send any more Kurdish Peshmerga to help them.

Another Yezedi fighter, Suleiman Khalaf, also called the commander to see when reinforcements would come: Sarbast was called, from the Peshmerga, but he said he was in Dohuk. I told Sarbast, "Thanks so much for running away and leaving us!" No Yezedi fighter interviewed could remember any Kurdish Peshmerga soldier in Tel Azer being either wounded or killed before their forces evacuated Tel Azer.

Christine van den Toorn, a reporter with The Daily Beast, was quoted as follows in the EKurd Daily Newspaper report of August 18, 2014: "Despite the danger and fear of attack, locals consistently were discouraged from leaving Sinjar by local KDP and Kurdish government officials who reassured civilians that the Peshmerga would keep them safe.

A local KDP official, whom we'll call Amina because of potential security threats she may face, says that higher-ups in the party told representatives to keep people calm, and that if people in their areas of coverage left, their salaries would be cut."

Sarbast Baiperi, head of the KDP's Branch in Sinjar, could be seen in KDP media and on Facebook posing with various weapons and claiming that "until the last drop of blood we will defend Sinjar." But Sarbast Baiperi was one of the first to flee Sinjar, according to several sources.

He rolled out of town the night before the attack had even started because he heard IS was on its way to the outlying villages of Seebaya and Tel Banat. And not only did he flee, but he fled in a single vehicle, telling no one but his guards.

Late the next morning when townspeople fled in panic only minutes ahead of the advancing IS fighters, Baiperi was waiting at the Tirbka checkpoint north of the mountain near to the Syrian border. Baiperi, unfortunately, was part of a greater trend.

First hand accounts from Sinjar paint a picture of withdrawal without a fight and without warning the local population. The first quiet retreat was in the southern villages, which bore the brunt of the initial attack.

Late into the night of Saturday, August 2, ISIS first launched mortars into Seebaya and Tel Banat, close to the militant group's positions in Baadj district.

It was at his time in the battle that Yezedi men, not Peshmerga, stood and fought thinking that the Kurdish forces would soon join in the battle. When they realized that wasn't going to happen, many tried to escape over the mountain.

While it is difficult at this point to estimate how many were killed, locals say the number was around 200. If the Yezidi men had known the Peshmerga would withdraw, they might have fled earlier as well. Alone, they were no match for the IS army.

North of the mountain, locals received no warning from Peshmerga or KDP and government officials regarding the attacks, said Amina, who worked for the party in that region. She heard about attacks from her aunt who lives south of the mountain and she called her sub-branch director.

She was told to stay calm and that there was no withdrawal. But when she called Sarbast Baiperi's guards they said he had left the night before and they themselves were already gone, and they confirmed the troop withdrawal.

Others from northern villages had similar stories: foggy information about the nature of the attacks south of the mountain, unaware of Peshmerga withdrawal. So it was as late as 10 a.m. on that Sunday, after fighting had been going on for hours south of the mountain, that people in towns north of the mountain like Khana Sor and Dugre started to leave.

Many families were only minutes ahead of ISIS. Ahmed, a 70-year-old man from Khana Sor, says he heard the first gun shots behind him just as he left town — and running and driving alongside the fleeing civilians were the Peshmerga forces.

As they drove down the one safe from north of the mountain toward Duhok, under firm Kurdish control, the Peshmerga abandoned each checkpoint, joining the exodus.

Soon the twin columns of refugee civilians and Peshmerga came under sporadic fire, but the Kurdish government forces by then were neither positioned nor inclined to fight back. Amina's cousin was shot in the hand. Bullets and ricochets blasted through car windows and windshields. There were Army and civilians fleeing together.

There were some Kurdish fighters who tried to stand their ground, but they were from neighboring Syria, members of the so-called People's Protection Units of a militia, affiliated with the Turkish-Kurdish PKK, that goes by the initials YPG. The group is famous for its many women warriors, and they were much in evidence fighting back against ISIS forces during the flight from Sinjar.

The announcement of the evacuation orders of the Peshmerga soldiers was not communicated in an orderly and timely manner over a public warning system. Such a system had never been built in the village, dependent as it was on ancient traditions and technology.

The people were lulled into the false hope that the Kurds were guarding them even long after the Kurds had abandoned the field to the safety of the Kurdistan Region.

Kurdistan Region's President Masoud Barzani announced on television that any Peshmerga responsible for the early evacuation of Sinjar District would be tried in a court of law. But no one was ever charged or brought to justice.

The Yezedis are the ones who paid the total price of their silent withdrawal. The Yezidi people felt deeply betrayed, misled by the Peshmerga about something vital to their survival.

Some imagined afterward that a conspiracy had formed among Kurds, Americans, and Arabs with an express intent to annihilate Yezidis. Yet the Kurds were making an orderly and reasonable decision to evacuate in the face of an overwhelming force. Their superior officers were just facing the facts that no one had adequately supplied them with arms to adequately resist such a powerful force.

Their failure lay in their misleading statements and failure to truthfully, rapidly, and widely inform the Yezidi people of the eminent danger, or in helping the Yezidis prepare in advance for evacuation during such an attack.

The Americans, far away, were struggling to get enough intelligence from the local scene and to jump through all the usual hoops in the complex U.S. political machinery before making a decision on how to approach the emergency.

The Shia Muslim Arabs ruling Baghdad were preoccupied with their own problems, not very interested in collaborating with Kurds, and Yezidis were not their highest priority.

There was no vast conspiracy against Yezidis except the sudden involvement of their supposedly moderate Sunni Muslim Arab local neighbors with ISIS, the beasts who were symbolically taking leads from their Army and awaiting the signal from their own gardens to join in and slit the throats of their neighbors and rape their daughters opportunistically.

The underlying problems were several, at the sad risk of oversimplifying: (1) the delay in foreign arms support directly to the Kurds, due to the unyielding interest of the U.S. in supporting federal Iraq against the Kurdistan Region's bid for independence, (2) the Arab Iraqi central government's failure to pass arms through to the Kurds for fears of strengthening their bid for independence, (3) the desire of Turkey to discourage Kurds in their restless eastern region from being inspired to seek independence from Turkey, and (4) the failure of all parties to recognize the Yezidi militia as a protective security force worthy of early and significant training, armament, and support against ISIS.

A stronger force of personnel and arms serving without the distraction of family members in their immediate area would have been more effective. All Yezidi fighters were inclined to protect the village at least as long as their lives and the lives of their families were not at ultimate risk, but before the job was done, some may have been willing to yield their positions to save themselves and their families.

Their choice to fight for a while and leave when overwhelmed was a prudent choice for men who had families on the battlefield.

CHAPTER FOUR

"MAYHEM"

" There is no flag large enough to cover the shame of killing innocent people"

Howard Zinn

They were hungry and exhausted from the night before. The sun had not yet come up and the early morning was met with sounds of gunfire. The screams and shots went on incessantly throughout the night. It had been so hot in early August, and no one could even think of sleeping. Every shot meant that someone was losing a family member.

Nadja's parents were busy trying to keep their faces in a casual mode as the state panic was setting in rapidly. Deep down inside they knew that their lives were about to change forever. But they could not predict the immediate outcome.

There were the sounds of helicopters and planes flying overhead. There was shooting coming from inside and outside the village. The people, young, old were scurrying everywhere. A man had ran to their house to warn them of the imminent danger.

He himself took off on foot to the mountain never to be seen again. It was 2014 and in the modern era of mankind, and no one would even remotely anticipate that this hideous, archaic form of violence would be forcibly advanced upon these peace-loving people… again.

It was the 12th Century being replayed and this time with modern day weapons. The latter years had the Yezidis sharing parts of their current village with Arab Muslims. This was a result of ISIS pushing most of the Kurdish people out of the area, and replacing these residents with ISIS sympathizers. The day before, one of the men had told them falsely that all was well and that they did not have to easy their families to leave.

The Yezidi Elders had believed him and told everyone not to worry and that they would be able to stay without any imminent harm. Little did they know that those giving out misleading and deadly information had already been paid by ISIS. What was at stake was the lives of young Yezidi women and the gold of the village, which was abundant. This would be after the men were condemned to death.

Now it was too late. Everyone that Nadja's family knew in the village was either on the road to the mountain or captured on the way or killed. By the time that had they had discovered that they have been lied to, every family was frantically hurrying to pack what they thought were the most critical and cherished items in their home.

A journey up a mountain meant that they had to pack light. They had to make difficult decisions about clothing, pictures and jewelry. In the end the decisions came down to exactly how much water could be brought along quickly.

Also, they had to make a quick plan of how to help the elderly many who were disabled. They had to be assisted up the steep mountain, or how many diapers or rags could be carried for babies.

But they we aware that timing was everything, and they had to move quickly or lose their very lives. ISIS was on the way and they had to make it to Mount Sinjar from their Village of Sinjar or Shingal as it was sometimes called.

This was the second time that they had packed. They had unpacked in hopes that ISIS would change their minds like they had done in El Kosh. They had totally turned back from this Christian village. They had no idea that it would not even be necessary, and that they would ultimately beg to remain alive.

There was no way to imagine what was in store for the people here in this village. It would be one of the the worst holocaust events in modern-day history.

The Yezidis had been aggressively hunted, but this time they would be slaughtered in a fashion foreign to warfare for the modern day. and their story would remain a scar on the entire world for decades to come.

The sounds of firearms and airplanes flying had really started at 3:00 am. In the morning they realized that every Yezidi family was gone. Only Muslim families were left. They ran to the neighbors and borrowed their truck to leave the village. People tried to set off toward the mountains, but were stopped by ISIS on the way.

The fighters were from other countries, not only from Iraq. They had big new cars. They were from Pakistan, Egypt, Saudi Arabia. They told everyone to get off the truck. Outside of the house was virtual mayhem. The scene was surreal. From a peaceful village where everyone hope for a smile and some news of a wedding to people running screaming and falling over dead bodies. The men had been executed one by one, their dead bodies laying where they had fallen.

The women and little girls were being separated from the boys and the young men. One little girl whose face Nadja would frequently remember was one of the neighbor's little girl.

This little girl, was only eleven years old. They raped her with no mercy. It was one of the saddest moments there in the village during those terrible hours. Finally, a young boy about 12 years old came to the house, and he said that his father and brothers had been killed. He was in a state of shock and there was no way to console him.

Nadja's little brother was curious and so Yousif, thinking that he was not in any immediate danger, ran outside to see just what was happening. He had returned quickly because all he could see was corpses of fallen men and young boys in their streets. With the block near them covered with dead bodies he had accidentally stepped across the body of his older cousin.

Dead villagers that were relatives friends covered the roads with their lifeless stares. There were corpses everywhere. Some had been there for many hours, and maggots and flies had now begun crawling in and out of their mouthes and noses.

These were people that Nadja's family had cried, laughed and eaten with, and they had all joined in the various villages celebrations throughout all of her young life.

Outside people were moving on the road and Nadja was surprised that that they were so many people in her village. Many of the accounts stated that more than 50,000 Yezidi people had fled their homes in their ancestral lands.

The people were forced to abandon their homes and flee to the mountain without any food or water. There thousands died on the mountain, and the ones who were left behind on near the mountain were massacred or captured.

Nadja was to learn that more than 5,000 women were taken to be used as sex slaves, with an estimated 2,000 women who would still remain in captivity. They would most likely never see their families again.

As they made their move to try to get out of their house and to the mountain, they came out only to discover that the city had been surrounded. The gunfire was closer now. People and trucks were being fired upon in the streets. While they were trying to pack, ISIS had already moved into the village. They were uncertain now what to do and escape seemed futile. Nadja's Family went back into their house to seek refuge and hear from someone that there was a safe way out of the village.

They stayed in their home for five hours waiting for a call on one of the mobile phones but no word came. It had already been too late for Nadja's family. They could not flee to the mountains. They would be trapped there in in the grips of ISIS in their own village until help could arrive from the Peshmerga.

Even if they could escape to the mountain it would only mean slow starvation for those whose could survive. The Sinjar Mountains lie near the Syrian border, and because the way into Kurdistan from inside Iraq is blocked by Sunni militants, the Yezidis hoped to cross the mountains and make their way to Kurdistan through an alternative route.

There was no new route, and there was no escape. Escape and hope was not to be the case for Nadja's family, however. Nadja could never forget that ominous knock on the door. There stood a number of ISIS militant troops. They took all 9 members of her family. They took them from the house one by one.

First they took her mother and her father. Then they proceeded to round up Nadja at her two small brothers and little sister. Her grandfather and grandmother were taken out separately. They were dragged like animals and placed across the street from their house.

Everyone that was brought outside who were still in the village were all screaming, crying and begging the militants not to harm them or their children. This was to no avail. The louder they screamed the worse the ISIS invaders' punishments continued. It was thought they enjoyed desecrating the lives of these peaceful people.

ISIS had arrived, and they had made their presence known with bloodshed. Nadja was trying to find some logic of the horrible circumstances that had overtaken her village. Her thoughts throughout the noise of the gunfire took her back to the sounds of her mother, Rooba's voice asking her and her little sister to help her prepare some things for a meal.

They bickered until one would surrender and begin to wash the vegetables or start boiling the water for the rice. The boys ran in and out of the house as they waited eagerly for dinner. Their father seemed always to be caught up in a conversation with the neighborhood men about new work and politics in Kurdistan.

Nadja had remembered his bravery to the end. Nadja would give anything to hear those voices once more and to help her mother in the kitchen again. Yet, she knew that she would not hear those beloved sounds again. ISIS terrorists had seen to that.

Shots rang out, and it was like a bad nightmare was happening while they were fully awake. Her father had been moved along with the other men as to form a group. He and the next door neighbor was shot and died together right in front of her and her family's eyes.

His body was made limp by a stream of bullets. His loving eyes had met hers as he fell to the ground. Those dying eyes would haunt her for the rest of her life She saw the pain, but they were eyes of bravery and comfort. Her father's body along with the others was discarded like old daily trash.

NASIMA

The invaders were organized for a military take over of a quiet mountain people who kept to themselves. There would have been no way to arm against them either mentally or with weapons. ISIS took each aggression and assault with the weight off all of Islam at stake.

Many of these men were relatives or very close friends of their family. Their history together was tragically stopped when the bullets were fired endlessly into the bodies at will on that horrible day. These victims had names, faces and families.

Many were slaughtered unmercifully and that may have been the mercy. Children were buried alive in small mass graves. Women were rounded up and carted off like cattle. There was no sparing of anyone as ISIS insisted that they were the chosen ones to carry on the "cleansing".

The next door neighbor who was shot with Nadja's father was killed because he had been a policeman. It made no difference to ISIS that he was an Arab. Everyone was a virtual target that day. The whole scene was so surreal but the most painful part for her and her mother was what happened after the guns had been turned on Nadja's little brothers.

When the oldest, Yousif, had broken away from her mother's arms. Even in the face of danger, he was so brave and still trying to protect his family. Nadja could not believe her eyes as Yousif stood up to Isis as though they were just a gang of his rowdy classmates.

He was shot immediately and Nadja could see his brain and bone fragments splattered and hit a nearby car. His young lean body hit the ground in a heap. This scene caused Nadja to be proud of her brother, and would break her heart for the rest of her life.

Her youngest brother, Walid, was suddenly being swept away and thrown into a vehicle with many other young boys. Some were crying and scared, while others were in total shock and dismay.

They had heard about other villages and were well aware that they were to be taken and trained for "service" with ISIS. Eventually Walid would be sent to the front lines against the Peshmerga when the fight came to Mosul.

Nadja did not know if she would ever see him again. He was eight years old. Her heart seemed to have left her body. But the demons controlling ISIS had still not inflicted enough pain.

There was the most heart wrenching moment for the rest of the surviving villagers to ponder. One man took Nadja's little blonde haired, blue eyed sister by the arm. He forcibly ripped her away from from Rooba's arms.

Then, another man pushed his way forward and they seemed to be fighting over Nasima. They seemed to be in dispute about which one would take her. This bought Nasima some precious minutes before the horror occurred.

Rooba was letting out bloodcurdling screams. She was being tightly held back, while it seemed that they would rip her little daughter apart. They tugged and tugged viciously at her little arms fighting over who would be the grown man to take the little blond girl.

Little Nasima was scratching at the air and blurting out howling screams for her mother. Then she began to scream for Nadja. Both remained helpless to help the little girl. They were held back at gun point and their arms were being held by ISIS militants.

These beasts were ready not only to take the village, but leave indelible marks of cruelty burned into each woman and child's memory forever. One of the men lowered his voice and said something that must have had an air of authority for the other man. He stopped his tussle over the child for a brief moment.

One more threat by the he man on the left suddenly let her go, and then with brute force the man, who won the argument began to tear off Nadja's little sister's clothes.

Then the unthinkable happened. The man who considered himself a victor, raped little Nasima in front of everyone still there. She was only 10 years old.

Rooba fainted and there was nothing that anyone could do to help this precious child, who had then been tossed to the ground like a sack of old garbage. The saddest part was that the man walked away with an insane smile as if to say to himself that he had conquered something or someone through an act similar to relieving one's self in a toilet.

The sad misfortunes of the Yezidis and the atrocious attacks on them on that frightful morning in August, brought them to their knees. The pain was indescribable.

There were countless the numbers of bodies on the streets. The whole village had been plundered after being ransacked for the gold owned by the brides. The scene was one the people read about only in books, or heard from their grandparents or elders.

Tears and screams were met with with disregard by ISIS. They kept everyone who had survived moving swiftly onto their next pitiful destination. The ones who had remained alive were gathered up like spoils of a war, most being separated from their own families.

They would soon be sold after moving to the nearby military camps of ISIS soldiers. They would be traveling numb without any words to reflect what they had just endured.

CHAPTER FIVE

"LIVING HELL"

" Let your plans be dark and impenetrable as night, and when you move, fall like a thunderbolt."

Sun Tzu

Nadja could not trust herself to believe that there would be any mercy mixed with one drop of human kindness. Not after all of the horrific events she had just witnessed. She had been shipped to Raqqa, Syria as no more than livestock or cargo.

The women were pushed, shoved, moved and loaded into the vehicles that were awaiting them. She was trying to crawl into the arms of her mother who was in the same vehicle as her and her little sister. It was not allowed.

When they threw the women and children into the truck they grabbed each one by their hair, they immediately tried to force them to wear a black abaya, chained their hands in front of them, placed blindfolds on the older girls and made them to ride for 12 long hours. There was no food or restroom breaks, only suffering.

There was such misery amongst them. If she could have chosen to comfort one person or the other, she could not have decided who it would be. Nadja sat startled in a state of helplessness. She could not remember when was the last time that she had eaten anything or drank of the fresh spring water of her mountain region.

To quench her thirsty, empty soul, she would have desired to bring peace to just one member of her family. Her little brother had been taken and she wondered whether or not he had slept or eaten. Who would laugh with him? Who would cry? Her mother was in a state of shock and her little sister was broken and bleeding.

Nasima laid on her side. She was confused, battered and bleeding, in the back of a strange truck. She was mumbling through her sobs, the faint but same words over and over. The only intelligible words Nadja could make out were the soft phrases in Kurdish, "Mommy why didn't you stop them?".

Rooba had lost her little girl. Nasima was still alive, but would be one of the walking dead forever. She was torn and wounded from the inside of her little body to the outside. No doctors would be able to help her in time. She would have to heal without cleaning or stitching her little scarred body.

There would be no future of picking flowers, falling in love or getting married someday for this precious little child. Her next days would be in anguish and torment. She had been treated like a woman and had no idea what that role was. This was all foreign to this little girl so there would be no way to explain to her what she had been used for.

Nadja knew in her heart that there had been such irreparable damage perpetrated on this sweet child. Each woman was suffering in ways that were there own. Husbands gone, sons killed or taken, and this right in front of their helpless eyes.

However, the reality played over in her mind that her personal tragedies far out weighed those of her surrounding community. This was happening to her family and her personal grief would not allow her to empathize with the neighbors.

A new day was breaking and it was simply impossible to describe what was happening to them. Riding the bumpy roads to Raqqa, after experiencing the shocking horrors of watching her family being destroyed by these animals, was simply more than she could bare.

She had to secure some kind of sanity so that she could help her little sister and her mother. They rode silent all thinking of a way out of their circumstances. They could not give up for the sake of their family and friends. who were now shoved into mass graves.

However, there was nothing or anyone who could have prepared Nadja and her mother, Rooba, for what was about to take place in their lives. They had lived nominally off of their own land and had not hurt a soul.

They had passed from a life of peace and simplicity at home, to the three of them being hurled into a sub-existence that would continue as Nadja's darkest night in her soul.

They had been so violently ripped from their peaceful village, and had to get prepared to be sold like the sheep that they had raised. They had even unknowingly passed by a building on their way to the compound that was designated as the sale area for these captured women and children.

The women who had ridden with them were also from their village. These were people that they had seen on frequent occasions at the market, but had never met them personally. Now they were sharing their dark fate together.

These were Christian women who had seen their husbands, brothers and sons decapitated. The militants used their deaths purely as propaganda to bring fear to the Westerners.

These memories would burn forever in their souls, as they could still envision the eyes that were staring wide open, that seemed to be pleading for mercy. These were the innocent eyes still crying within the severed heads. This included the young men who were on the verge of marriage or opening business with their fathers. Just days before their demise they had experienced joy with their whole life in front of them. They loved them even more.

These women from a neighboring village, however, had been taken in the earlier raid were seemingly strong and strangely hopeful. These women seemed to be involved in some kind of praying, although it was in another language. They would say in unison at the end of each sentence the word, "Amen", so Nadja instinctively bowed her head with them. After all, it couldn't hurt, and since they were not Muslim she would commune in their sanctity.

She thought them to be some sect of Christians in whom the Yezidis had no problems. Nadja respected their willingness to pray even at the risk of being shot. And later Nadja would notice that one thing was quite odd...none of them would be sold into the hands of the waiting buyers. This would later puzzle Nadja.

When they had crossed over into Syria. It was in Raqqa where they took most of the women initially. They were all forced from the truck into a big compound. There was no air circulating and I was so hot that they could barely breathe. There were women with little children.

Their babies were crying because of hunger and thirst. Many of the infants were not yet potty trained and there no diapers or milk. Then they were shoved and hoarded into the place where they would be kept. They longed only to find a place to rest from the invasion, being abducted and then the long hard ride.

Many just collapsed in corners in an exhausted heap. Others stood with their faces against the wall staring and sobbing. Some made no sounds, but moaned and seemed to have passed into a state into oblivion, lost in the harrowing past moments.

Nadja tried to find her mother and Nasima, but they had been quickly led away to separate quarters. Older children were scared and screaming at the top of their lungs, with no one to help them.

Then, they heard the big door slam, and the lock loudly clicking as if to mock their circumstances further. The echo of the bolt being shoved rang through the compound for several seconds. It was like a cold knife going in and out of their hearts.

During the chaos, their captors silently made it plain to their innocent captives, that in no uncertain terms, their lives, their families, their culture and religion was under siege. This meant that everything that they had once held dear was now completely in the hands of the ruthless ISIS invaders.

They were forced to stay in the filth of the compound for several days with each day only eating one dry biscuit and very little water. Bathing consisted of a little water, no soap and a dirty rag. Most women just passed on this prospect. The idea, also, was that if they refused to bathe, their captors may find them reprehensible.

They instinctively knew exactly what was next on the agenda. Their captors knew no limits, so they considered physical enslavement, beatings and other cruelties part of their normal day. The exchange for a little food, water and a filthy bed with no sheets or blankets would be their virginity and for the older women, their honor.

The smells in and around the compound were horrendous. It was an odor of a cross between mildew and old sewage, and it didn't help that it was dimly lit and it was very hot in August. If there was no breeze, then the conditions were slightly tolerable. When the hot winds blew, they were breathing in pure stench.

They kept throwing out commands but in Arabic. Most Yeziti women refused to adhere to any of their demands, as they did not speak the language. It easy especially difficult to try and understand meanings, when it was totally unintelligible as the militants were screaming and spitting their commands.

No one could understand the various dialects in Arabic except for the Christian girls, who understood a little. Muslim garb was thrown at them, and they were commanded to put it on, to cover so as to pay homage to their new forced religion. They all refused what they believed to be the first step in conforming to the radical ideals of the militants.

Following the horrible initiation to compound living, and the refusal by the women to adorn the black garb, some of the militants arrived shortly thereafter with a visitor. A man strode into the compound and looked the women and children over as to view cattle and what price they could bring.

It was all about money for ISIS. They had ultimately been defeated in Kirkuk, IRAQ which was where the oil fields were located, so they were always looking for new ways to fund their war efforts. Selling people was one of their ways to make money and they enjoyed going from village o village stealing, gold historical artifacts, and PEOPLE.

The man who slithered into the rooms throughout the compound was considered a holy man by the militant soldiers, and they seemed to give him the deepest respect even when he barked orders at everyone all around him.

It was assumed that he had all of the religious answers to any questions that would be posed, and if he didn't know he could make it up on the spot. He carried a book in one hand and a thick stick in the other. This was an Imam and this was hid duty.

He was more than a religious leader. This man was an radical extremist who was also a certified ISIS beast. He raped and tortured the women right along with the soldiers in the name of his god. He had come to the compound to sexually harass the women and force their religious conversion without any more resistance.

He swung the stick with one hand high in the air to intimidate those who had been incarcerated by the angry militants. He was going to convince them with a good beating and reading out of his prayer book simultaneously.

He wanted notches on his religious holster one way or another. He insisted that everyone say the words that he was spouting and then they would be magically converted to Islam and it's suffering and demeaning of women.

The women still refused and were, in turn, beaten. They were not badly bruised on their faces or on their hands, as they would bring in more money for the seller if they were fair-skinned, clean and not blemished.

After all, these were the "fresh picks" of the Yezidi villages, and they would bring a very handsome price from wealthy Arab businessmen. They soon were going to be needed to be inspected from head to toe for the "sale."

The buyers were almost always wealthy older Arab Sunni Muslim men from the local areas occupied by ISIS. The girls were oftentimes sold and resold repeatedly while in captivity, their "ownership" being passed from one older man to another.

In each transfer, there is the humiliating and sickening experience of being looked over by several men or many men, usually in Mosul, Iraq, or Raqqa, Syria, with gawkers appraising the woman or girl with their eyes, touching her, running their hands over her body in a way that violated her even further.

Their mouths would be forced open to have a look at their teeth. Bad dental hygiene was a sign that pain would follow and no one wanted to engage in helping find dental or medical care.

The ISIS soldiers behaved like a bunch of wild beasts. The lined up buyers who drank tea and talked over the live merchandise. They clapped and jeered when the Yezidi women and girls were presented. They were considered prime merchandise.

They laughed and joked about what they would do to each one and since they spoke Arabic instead of Kurdish the sting did not penetrate the women's hearts as much as the laughter stung their ears.

But, their horrible treatment and mocking chuckling like little school girls was an undeniable sign that these men were truly sick and depraved animals. They enjoyed their time together trading and treating the women like you would at a sheep sale or a furniture auction.

They had showed no mercy and certainly no remorse as these women to them were just objects to be beaten and raped. Often the smaller children of a woman were sold with their mothers, and occasionally subjected to pedophilic violations of their bodies and rapes. Mothers had to stand by and witness their children being taken to rooms and raped, while scrubbing some foreign family's floor.

They were silenced with brutal beatings and worse. Self-righteous Muslim men often prayed before or after raping the girl or woman, and sometimes explained how they were saving her soul by making her Muslim through sex rather than her willing conversion.

She may even be considered a Muslim just because a man forced himself upon her. An automatic conversion, if you will, while he raped her of all dignity. She was forced her to accept her shame, and wear it like a badge, but through his religious brainwashing was relieved of any guilt.

The fighters would tell them it was their right to "marry" (rape) them as spoils of their involvement in the war. The older men would make the women or girls false promises about houses, money, and care for their children, then sell them off when they grew tired of them.

Because the rapists routinely forced the use of contraceptives on the young Yezidi girls and women, few were impregnated, around five percent. In cases of pregnancy, abortions were sometimes forced, or the woman would be violently hit in the abdomen in an attempt to cause spontaneous abortion.

Very few gave birth to the children of terrorists, whether before or after they came home. Their long-term attitude toward the children of terrorists as members of the family remained to be seen, and the attitude of their neighbors and communities toward the children, though muted by shock and disbelief at first, was likely to emerge later in a multitude of negative ways.

The prices for ransom started at around $200, but climbed to as high as $1,300 by early 2016, with some outliers such as a beautiful 11 year-old girl who was reportedly sold for $2,000. The ransoms grew higher and higher as Mosul was going to be invaded by Kurdish, IRAQI and other armies coming in from all over the world.

Some families paid ransoms without the involvement of the Kurdish government, and some organizations claimed to have ransomed people without involving the government.

There were precious men who risked their lives to go into Mosul and "buy" the sex slaves as though they were making the purchase for themselves. They were angels who took it upon themselves to purchase freedom as many captives as humanly possible.

Most ransoms were paid by family members. But, Nadja had no one that could buy her mother, her little sister, and herself from out of this living hell.

The Kurdish government had a policy of repayment of such ransoms, with some limitations and with proof of payment with their involvement. In some cases, the Kurdish government quietly paid the ransoms themselves, which is not unusual for governments in this era, but had been eschewed in the West in previous decades.

Then after several days, each and every woman and child were dragged into a makeshift mosque which was outside. At least they could freely breathe a little. It was extremely hot and they were made to stand there for what seemed like hours.

The children were becoming sick. Each woman was trying to hold on to what ever life she could. Rooba was brought out separately to the slave auction, not with the other women.

Nadja was numb until she saw her mother and Nasima. That was exactly what it turned out to be. Nasima and another little girl was amongst them and they were sold right away. The other little girl was only 4 years old. It was said that she would "marry at nine".

But the buyer could use his own discretion as to when the "marriage" would take place. She like Nasima was very beautiful with blonde hair and gorgeous green eyes.

There was not a drop of emotion involved in the transaction. Men were coming in from, Yemen, Saudi Arabia and other countries to "purchase" those women and young girls who had been captured. One woman was sold and the buyer brought her into a house where two other men also lived. She had only desired to be with her sister. She begged him and pleaded that they may stay together.

His answer was to hit her with his pistol on my head until she was bleeding. They did not even bring her to a hospital, instead they brought her back to the prison while she was still unconscious. Her sister was sold three days later, and her and her sister were heart broken. They were reunited later only when she and her sister were sold to the very same people, along with seven other girls.

Another woman was sold along with her cousin who was still a little child. Neither had any family besides each other, and no one had any idea where the little girl's mother had ended up.

This made the little girl even more precious to her, and she felt such a need to sacrifice her own life, and protect her sweet innocence from what was to come. She had felt such a responsibility to carry her through this hell, and attempt to keep her from the savages who considered the lives of the Yezidis as cheap as dirt.

This went for the sellers as well as the buyers. These were the brokers of broken dreams and the humiliation. These were innocent and young human lives. These young women and little girls were robbed of any thought of a functioning future.

The story was told by one courageous young girl, at the auction whoa only wanted to protect her little cousin. She had paid a heavy price indeed. There would be one hideous scenario after another to come for her.

Finally, the man who decided to buy them both saw in her a fire, and he thought that he would take the challenge to break her. He was married. He kept insisting that he sleep with the older girl to make sure that he converted her to Islam. She would not cooperate in the least. Then he tried to rape her but she fought with all her might.

She would not allow him to take what was left of her dignity. She continued to refuse him, and kept reminding him that he was already married. He threatened her with many weapons, beat her, hit her with a gun to the head. She held strong and because he was a busy trader and didn't have time for such a task, finally sold her and her tiny cousin to someone else.

The next house was even worse. The wife of the man was vicious. She beat them both when he was out, because she was jealous and knew he was determined to sleep with the the beautiful older girl.

The man was constantly trying to persuade her that sleeping with him would not only make her a full fledged Muslim, but she would have certain new privileges in the house. She could not fathom what they could possibly be as she did ALL of the housework.

She was cleaning the house, doing all of the laundry and preparing every meal daily for his family. She was beaten by his wife and worked without mercy. This was due to the fact that there was now are young woman in the house that her husband wanted to have sex with.

He was obsessed with the notion that he was going to have sex and convert someone to Islam at the same time. This brought the wife both sorrow and anger.

The young girl had to witness the unthinkable. Her little cousin was beaten by the cruel wife daily. She refused to allow the little child's diaper to be changed. Once it was for a week at a time. She beat her and beat this little one, and then filled the little child's mouth with peppers just because she was unable to speak Arabic.

Then, she as tiny as she was, was locked in a room with the door opening only to give her small pieces of food with a sip of water. The child was so traumatized by this bitter treatment and she was literally starving to death. This went on for five months....until they were sold again.

Then another girl told of her horrible encounters. She was twitching as she recanted her horrible ordeal. She hd gone from Tal Afar to Mosul and then Raqqa, where she was now with Nadja. She was sold by another soldier to a high ranking officer in ISIS.

She too was beaten brutally by the wife of the extremist. She could not persuade the wife that had no interest in her husband, but it didn't matter. When he was not around the woman went into tirade.

She had lied about one of the children who was sold with her and had said that she was her little sister. Although they were not related she cared for the little three year old girl.

The woman then proceed to hang the little girl out of the window holding her by her ankles. The little child screamed and squirmed. Then suddenly, when the woman tuned to the older girl to

On one afternoon after the woman had one of her fits she ordered this girl to bring the child to her. She reluctantly went and got her from the other room. The woman was in a tizzy and grabbed the child from her, shook her and then drug her to the window.

The little one was screaming and trying to break free. She was swept up in a fit of rage by this woman. It was not enough for them to cook, clean and be brutalized daily. She wanted revenge.

They were on the fifth floor of the house. The woman scolded the older one scold once more about her husband and her wanting to sleep with her. While she was screaming at the older one, the leg of the child slid from her hands and she say her tiny cousin drop. She was killed instantly and the older girl went blank.

As she told the story the twitching grew more noticeable and Nadja saw that it was apparent that the girl was psychologically damaged for life. This is how she was returned to Raqqa, broken and not even desired by ISIS, which for all intents and purposes was maybe a blessing in disguise.

When Nadja her mother, and little sister had been taken from the village by ISIS, it was whispered in the truck that they would be sold and taken away to other countries. That was the only tribulation that they could try to somehow prepare themselves for. They would be constantly be forced, without success for ISIS, to convert to Islam.

They knew that these strangers were brutal in their forcing themselves physically on young Yezidi girls. There was no love in the language of the ISIS militants. Sex was one of their weapons, and until Nasima had been ruthlessly attacked.

Nadja had no concept of rape. She had no real concept of sex at all. It was never discussed their household. She had a teenage crush on a certain boy in the village, but those dreams were that of a little girl singing, laughing and picking flowers.

She had witnessed her father gently kiss her mother on her forehead many times, yet she had not envisioned a tiny romantic kiss for herself, as there was no real time to romanticize.

ROOBA

Nadja had seen her mother only the first few moments when they arrived at the compound, but she was not allowed to speak to her. During a time outside some days later, Nadja saw her mother and noted how she had aged in only a few days.

Their eyes did meet and hot tears flowed from both of them. No words were exchanged. This was the only communication that they would allow themselves, so that the punishments would not be worse. They were separated again until they could only catch glimpses of each other at the "place of the sale".

Nadja had never, ever seen Rooba so weak and torn. She could stand up to most anything in the village. Nadja had witnessed her mother giving birth to the youngest children and the family.

Rooba held up under adverse conditions in their village and there were no doctors to advise them in case of sickness or childbirth. With each baby she grew stronger and stronger. Nadja was her little rock.

She had not only been taught by Rooba, but was so willing to put her play time on hold to learn how to care for the household. She had sweetly cared for the family while Rooba would heal and bond with each one of the new babies. She worshipped her mother's strength, and courage.

Yet, both Rooba and Nadja could only stand by and watch as they were introduced to the same living hell as the others. Rooba had to succumb to the fact that her children were all but gone. Taken and tortured with a helpless mother that could only look on.

"How could she have allowed this to happen to her family", is all that she could think about? But, when Nadja could see her in the area around the compound, she could understand why Rooba had lost all hope her heart.

When Nadja would be near Rooba, her sweet mother would just look away in fear. Her eyes showed that she was drowning in a sea of anguish, helpless to help herself or her daughter. She was unable to come to the rescue of her daughters or herself and, she chose to sheepishly look down following their brief glance.

Nadja was worried about Rooba as it was apparent that she was so overwhelmed with such a sense of loss and she had never been acquainted with such shame. What was worse is that Rooba had two children out "there" somewhere whom she could not hold. She refused to believe that she would never see them again.

Her youngest son was taken at gun point on that treacherous morning. Then, shortly after arriving in the compound, Rooba watched as a man who was well over 50 years old had spotted little Nasima in the "sale".

He seemed to lick his lips as he was so eager to purchase this little angel. He hoisted Rooba's baby child into his vehicle. Rooba felt her heart leave her body.

Nasima had been raped publicly, lived though bleeding profusely and now this. She was just a child, but now no longer a virgin so she would be subjected to all of the ongoing sexual atrocities that the other women had to experience.

Nasima was not allowed to be with her mother, but had been in the care of other women in the compound. The separation was as painful as watching her being tortured by an animal.

This child had not received any comfort from her mother's arms since Sinjar. She was only a little child and she was feeling so confused and so abandoned by this time. It was almost too much to bear for Rooba and Nadja.

But still the very worst was yet to come to this once happy and stable family. These innocent women and children were treated as no more than ostracized criminals. So many others were selected and carried away to unknown destinations and houses. They were purchased and mocked.

The women in the compound were led out as cattle everyday, but not only to be sold but to watch their family and friends be carted away.

There was not a shred of humanity or dignity in the sellers or the buyers. The buyers had innumerable motives. Some loved torture and some just loved a clean house.

There was no way to determine what the fate of each woman or child would ultimately be. Nadja and Rooba had not been sold but were probed at each sale until they were sore.

Rooba and Nadja were reeling as they were led back to the compound separately. Ten year old Nasima had been sold for a very high price. There was no discussion possible, and they were almost relieved that they did not have to verbally survey how shattered their lives were, and the burning pain in their hearts.

They could not afford the attempt to bring their souls together to touch what had happened to them. Their heads fell like heavy weights. No words could explain the torment that was pored throughout their lives so ruthlessly, and at what seemed to be at a moment's notice. Both separately yet at the same time quietly wondered what had they done to deserve this heinous sentence.

Rooba had only known the father of her children. No other man had ever entered her heart or her bed chamber. Her father gave her wings to laugh and fly when she was just a little girl. The arranged marriage of her parents had so many wonderful occurrences.

The memories went on and on with her now dead husband, Zidan. Their love was what they both had needed. He was older, but so kind and gentle to her. Some of the men had beaten their wives in the village, but she had never experienced one day of even one cruel word with Zidan.

He really loved her and they both strove to make their house a real home with their beautiful little family. Most of the Yezidi families had numerous children and the men had numerous wives.

As a young wife, Rooba had only knew a life and routine of peace and gentleness. Her children had eyes that smiled and this made her heart glad. Solitude was better than gold as far as Rooba was concerned.

Rooba had grown up in peace and had just desired the same thing for her family. She knew how to be a wife and mother, but there was nothing in her present or past that could prepare her to lose the only part of life she clung to; her family and friends.

She could not believe the unspeakable horrors that had met her family just days before. And yet, it seemed that these days had lasted well over a thousand years.

The hours lingered on and there was pain at every turn. She only desired to at least let her thoughts remain with Nadja for as long as she could, because knowing that she was nearby would bring a little comfort. They had stolen the innocence of little Nasima right before her eyes. Now they had stolen another child from her.

Rooba knew that Nasima would not return to her. She held on tightly to the visions of her as a normal little girl, and hoped at least that she would remember to have in her heart a love like no other...her love, a mother's love.

Her only option left would be to choose to dwell on the fact that Nadja was a few walls from her. They could feel the beat of each other's hearts, although they felt a million miles apart. They would both seek some rest.

She tried to sleep but she tossed and turned thinking about the bodies of her husband and son. She wondered if her smaller children were eating. She wondered where they had been laid to rest. She longed for some kind of peace, some solace. But, there was nothing of the kind coming her way in her near or distant future.

The world kept turning and not to Rooba's advantage. Rooba was immediately separated from Nadja and Nasima. She could not remember not having them near her.

What was worse, however was that her little Nasima had been taken by a complete stranger to only God knows where. Yet, Rooba knew in her heart that it would surely be a foreign and non-compassionate country for a little Yezidi girl.

They would not allow her to see Nadja, and Rooba would plead with whoever would dump her small portion of food and water into her "living area". She screamed and even tried to speak to them in a soft tone of voice.

They ignored her as if she didn't exist. She was scarcely being kept alive and she did not know why. She was older than most of the girls there, but ISIS had plans for her. She would not be sold because she had the markings of a wife and mother.

A few light wrinkles and weathered hands made her a target for the soldiers in the compound to use her any way that they saw fit. She dared not think about the days and dark circumstances that were awaiting her.

Her heated tears however, were for her daughter, Nadja. She would not cry for herself, but for a child who had never known a man, or the cruelty that unwanted sex would bring without the slightest possibility of ever knowing real love. Rooba chose to remember Zidan's arms.

However, Rooba's horrific nightmare was just beginning. On a morning several days following the separation from her children, Rooba had been taken to the "officer's quarters" of the compound. There she was thrown into the worst degrading conditions anyone, especially a woman, could ever imagine.

Just a few days before she had been enjoying the fruits of the life of living in the the village. She was a loving wife, mother and a bright light to her family. She was loved and respected by the villagers.

They only knew Rooba to be strong and a great example of humor and dignity. She had never sat on her mobile phone to gossip or bring strife, but was ready with encouragement and great counsel for a community of women just like herself.

Although she was the mother of four children, she had worked hard all of her life. She followed all the ways of her mother. She got up early and had cared lovingly for her husband and children.

There were the usual daily struggles of sick children, the flocks growing, and husbands trying to make business to care for their families. She never had a day that she did't contribute to the welfare of her family.

She gave gentle orders from her bed while bearing her children. She was magnificent and though she was devastated and dropped into the compound, she still held her head up high.

Her wisdom was sought out by the wives and Rooba took great care to take as much time with everyone as she could. She loved to hear from those who needed to be heard.

She had not afforded herself the luxury of wondering why she was brought to the soldier's quarters. But she would soon learn that she was supposed to make her living quarters in another part of the compound. She was told to gather up her meager bedding.

She would learn that there was an ISIS soldier who had lost his lower legs in a battle. The man sat in a makeshift wheel chair. It served as his mobility and toilet at the same time. He was bitter and angry, and his military life was over. He would sit and see how far he could urinate across a room.

He refused to learn to walk with any prosthesis and he defecated and urinated on himself continuously. His legs had a putrid smell from the infection that had set in. The man's bandages were dirty and over used.

The irony was that he had stepped on a mine that his own ISIS brethren had previously planted. He was taken back to the compound bleeding and in pain. It was then that his brutal comrades showed him their real true colors. He got to witness the lack of sympathy that his fellow soldiers heartlessly exhibited.

A young soldier, who was a relative of the injured soldier had begged the ISIS soldiers not to shoot him and put him out of his misery. He was just a broken down burden, no more than a wounded dog, that they had no regard for.

He was treated with no more consideration than that of trash that needed to be burned. But, the relative implored them to show some mercy and promised that he would care for him, but the concern and lasted no time and the wounded man was completely abandoned.

These young radical soldiers had no experience in helping each other. Their only cause was killing and pillaging in the name of a religion that they rarely even opened their book to consult. They seemed to make up any and all rules from their book as they went along.

Those who knew what lay on the other side of the door could not any longer bring themselves to enter the contaminated room. He was not only uncooperative but he was truly ungrateful. Even ISIS, who didn't possess their souls, were not void in the needing of some kind of appreciation.

They had simply turned their backs and ignored their comrade's needs until they spotted Rooba as she entered the compound. A wife, a mother who still had a soft beauty about her. Suddenly, Rooba would have her world turned upside down in ways no woman in her prior circumstances could comprehend.

Rooba gathered her things, the clothes on her back and her dirty blanket and was hauled of to another part of the compound. She had been taken from what were already repulsive conditions in another area, and placed in a room that had odors that were so toxic, no human could tolerate them, but ISIS was not human.

They demanded codes of cleanliness for everyone else, but they had their own sub standards of living. Every place that they had taken was left a scorge, filthy and in the end destroyed. This compound reflected their evil and contaminated ways.

The soldier was no different. He had to have sat in the filth for many days, maybe weeks. She could not believe that she was predetermined to suffer in such a sick and twisted way.

She didn't waste any time, however, cleaning up the horrid mess, as the quicker she attended to the excrement the better it would be for her. She knew that there was no way out. Rooba immediately vomited all over the already filthy floor.

Rooba, Nadja's precious mother, a kind and creative soul became the recipient of serving such a filthy, disrespectful beast. After she had scrubbed the room as clean as she could with little water and no bleach, a new directive was forced upon her.

She was not only forced to bathe him, but then he demanded that she perform the lewdest of sex acts with this vulgar human being up to three times a day. If he were cleaned the act of being raped by him was not quite as bad, but he made it a point to spread the waste so that she would have to be degraded time and time again during the clean up process.

The soldiers had laughed as they pushed Rooba into the room with him. It was her punishment for being a woman who was not a virgin, and had no real value outside of someone to mock. She had become their sport. She almost fainted from the filth and smells. He defecated right in his chair as she was sent in.

The room had old urine stains on the walls and the floor. His legs had developed an infection and he smelled horrible. He still barked commands, pointed and screamed as if he were still some powerful militant soldier.

He had lost both of his lower limbs, but that made no difference. He would make it a point to drop things on the floor. He would call for Rooba to come over, and then when she got close he would grab her by the hair. He wasn't angry man due to his rejection and he took it out on Rooba.

He would attack her and then rape her repeatedly. She's then was expected to put him back in the chair after he had beaten and assaulted her on the stained and filthy floor.

After many weeks she would try to outsmart him and use her foot to pick up the object, but he would grab her by the back of her dress, move his hands up to her hair, and then pull himself out of the chair using her hair.

She was punished even more for trying to avoid him. These deplorable acts went on for almost 6 moths in Rooba's short life, but that was 6 months too long .

Rooba was a strong and resilient woman. She was facing each day with tears but with the courage of a lioness. She would not let him win. She refused to allow him to think that he was any better than an Yezidi wife and mother.

She even tried to picture in her mind who had given birth to this animal. She could not imagine his growing up years. But she had finally had enough. She seemed to have lost all that was dear to her, but she had the power to decide if this sick behavior was going to be perpetrated on her any longer.

That is when she spotted the pipes and she never took her eyes off of her blessed escape mode. They were above the mat where she slept. She had never noticed these pipes before. They were not only visible but beckoned her to a place of peace and dignity.

They looked strong at both ends and were sealed seamlessly into the concrete. There was an old chair in her room and two filthy sheets that they would not allow her to wash. She pulled up the chair to see how high the pipes were and would she be able to reach them.

She could not touch them with her hands, made a decision to tie the filthy sheets together. She climber down and made a freedom knot. This knot would secure her exit from this monstrous place, and to maybe see her son and husband again. She couldn't believe that she had not thought of this idea before.

Rooba made her own version of the slipknot and then proceeded to throw the long end over the pipes. She formed a makeshift noose and slipped it gently over her head. She kicked the chair aside and died seeing her children playing by the mountains of her home.

There is no doubt that human beings are resilient when they have to be, but at gun point they only have two choices; comply or die. She knew that her life was cheap and maybe she could have tried to keep on living for Nadja. It is nothing short of a miracle as to what humans can endure when counting their own torture insignificant when they truly love another.

Rooba endured the worst that one day she might be finally rescued. She could now hold all of her children in the vastness of eternity. Nadja would have to understand and not blame her for leaving the subhuman conditions.

Maybe she too one day could go free. Rooba didn't get to realize her dream of one day finding her beloved Nasima and Walid, but her new found freedom cost her attacker his imaginary control and power over such a gracious soul. She had won.

TRAPPED

Nadja had been informed by one of the other girls of her mother's death. She almost sensed relief. She was ambiguous about how to feel about her mother taking her own life, but that was the Rooba Nadja knew and loved.

What her mother had chosen to do caused her to love and respect her precious Rooba more than ever. She even secretly envied her courage. A woman of valor could not continue to service such an abominable excuse for manhood with her kindness and strength.

How her mother had endured that filthy beast for that period of time, she could not begin to imagine. She would not allow herself think about her mother's final days of forced rape and sick encounters with that cold-blooded monster , but instead chose to just remember her mother's loving acts of teaching and care to her father and the rest of the children.

She could not picture her mother with another man, but the reality was her mother had lived in such a terrible nightmare, and Nadja swore secretly to herself that she one day would take her own revenge. After all, it was her mother and her dear family that had suffered such tremendous loss.

Many nights had passed since Nadja had first entered this hell. She was truly all alone except for the soldier who was now standing over her in her room. He was drunk and she was weak.

He had made his way into the compound, a stranger to her and the other girls, and he had entered Nadja's little space where she slept on a dirty mattress with no sheet.

She was delirious for lack of food or water. She was so weak and exhausted that she could not raise her head up to see the face of the man. She was grieving for her family and at the same time being starved by ISIS, Sometimes there was only one piece bread a day with a little water.

She could see his frame, however and he was tall and very well built. All of them were older who were "officers" and allowed their pick of the young girls captured and thrown into the compound. His eyes flashed a hatred that penetrated her bones.

He wanted to begin her conversion with a violent indoctrination, and he began screaming some things at her and Arabic. He demanded that she bathe and began to tear off her dirty clothes.

Nadja violently refused his advances, then his impatience forced him to grab her by the throat and fling her onto the old mattress in the corner of the room. What was unusual was that he was going to attempt to rape her without her bathing. This took her by surprise. He spread her legs and placed a knee on one of her legs. It was so painful and she fought to get away.

He took his free hand and grabbed her by her hair and then began to put out his cigarette on her back. He kept his other hand over her mouth so she could not irritate him with her screams. He was absorbed in only one thing. She was a beautiful Yezidi girl, and he was going to spoil her for the rest of the takers.

Suddenly to his dismay, a loud type of alarm went off. It meant that every soldier would be called to the common area of the compound. The chaos outside was totally unanticipated, and Nadja was grateful beyond words for the abrupt interruption.

Nadja could hear loud voices and chaos in the yard of the compound. It was told to her later that several girls were trying to escape all at once. This would save Nadja from the advances of the man who had entered her room, but not for long. She knew that he was on a mission and would soon return.

Nadja was brought outside along with the other women and children who had just been sleeping. Nadja realized that she could barely walk because what had taken place in her "sleeping area". She was hurt from the scuffle.

Her legs were trembling from fear, and she noticed that she had been wounded by the man who determined to have his way. He had scratched her so deeply that she was pouring blood out of a wound, but along with this her period had started unexpectedly.

She was cramping and hurting from the assault. Blood was coming from several places, but she didn't yet, have to endure the memory of this man mauling her sexually.

Now the women and children who had already been awakened and brought out to the common area could see what the commotion was all about. There were about seven girls laying out on the ground with their hands tied with cables. The Imam showed up again to inquire into the situation at the compound.

He had been called and was told that they were bringing back some of the young girls who had escaped. He was energized as he again got to display his power. The girls who had tried to escape were brought back to the compound, bound, filthy and dirty.

They had been dragged through the dirt and were severely dehydrated. It was apparent that their quest for freedom had taken them far away from they compound. They had with all of their hearts for many miles.

The Imam began to beat them with what looked like a thick extension cord and he did not let up. They were beaten within the inch of their very lives. Each woman and child had to witness the viscous savage brutality and it was done publicly so all could see what would happen to them by example if they ever tried to get away.

They were given a lesson exactly as to what to expect if they tried to escape. Their screams were muffled when the Imam would cover their mouths, then he ordered the gun butts to strike their skulls.

When the other women who were standing by crying went near to help them, and try to bandage their wounds, they were warned to leave them alone until they were further ordered. The brave young girls laid outside injured and cold all night. Two of them died from the head wounds.

The soldiers were livid as they had lost money. This was their money that they had to place in a grave wrapped in a dirty sheet. They were nameless and worthless to ISIS and these precious souls would be remembered by these women only. Their memories would be honored as they were brave and attempted to possess their freedom at any cost. This made them furious.

More punishment was handed out randomly and Nadja fell victim. With what extra strength the Imam had left he beat several other girls. He then warned everyone who remained in the compound. Girls were handed over to the soldiers as gifts and their rapes were vicious. They were shared between other soldiers and the beatings only continue.

Everything changed that day for the worse if it get any worse. Nadja scared, bruised and bleeding crawled back to the compound. She could not walk after being beaten following being brutalized by the man who came in and injured her arms and legs.

She briefly looked up from the ground, thought of her mother's flight out, and knew she was trapped there with no other place to flee. She did to want to lie on the ground wounded or become conspicuous. She wanted to hide and not bring any attention to herself.

She was now more determined than ever that she would not bathe as this was the only weapon she had to ward off the animals that wanted to steal her youth. She was deathly afraid of what or who awaited her there in the area that she was assigned to. She pulled down another one of the soiled and filthy little mattresses that were heaped one upon another.

She noticed how pungent the odors were after being outside for a time. The room stank with body odors and semen. Although, Nadja was a child and could not distinguish one smell from another, she knew these were male adult odors.

She longed to run and just take a bullet in her back. Maybe she would just die quickly, but if she were injured there would be no one to help her. She remembered the others in the compound and without regard for herself, she gave up her idea of an honorable suicide.

She desired to stay with them. She had grasped and held tightly to the idea, with all of her being, that one day they would all connect with the courage they cradled inside, and seize an opportunity to flee these horrible circumstances.

She would wait knowing that her suffering would not compare to the day when she could run and keep on running. If she waited for her chance her freedom would only be that much sweeter. She returned and just settled into a corner. She sobbed and nodded off dreaming of a new day.

THE RAPE

Nadja had fallen into a deep sleep for the first time in many months. With all that had befallen her she felt an urgency to now leave part of the past behind. She wanted how do mind to slip into the memories of her childhood, like someone finding a hidden treasure.

And on that particular night she had ethereal visions of her family as she dozed off. Her mind was in such a relaxed state and the images were so pleasing. She could see every detail of her beloved mountain homeland.

They all seemed to be sitting on the floor in their small home eating an evening meal and she could even, in her vivid dream, take in the aromas of her mother's cooking.

She saw the dress of many colors that her little sister wore and heard her little brothers planning their next outing with the sheep. For them it had always been an adventure, not a chore. They ran back herding the sheep and brought along with them agates and artifacts to compare from ancient settlements.

They would place small cups and clay fragments of old plates with the ones that they had previously found. They would discuss who they thought the people had been in days gone by.

These little relics were common, as so many villages in their area had come and gone. They were all that was left to tell the stories of a people lost in invasions.

Suddenly, Nadja was awakened by the same man who had come to her sleeping area before. This time he had invaded her only place of privacy while she was in a deep sleep. This man was a coward. He had been watching her outside of her door.

He had scoped out and plotted against his innocent prey carefully since the last time he had launched his savage attack on her. She was completely defenseless, but in his mind she had to be conquered. Nadja gasped as she was awakened by this animal grabbing her by one of her the feet.

He pulled her from her sleeping mattress and slid her across the dirty floor. He whipped her body like a limp rag doll into a vacant room. She knew that he was not only back, but he was in a tyrannical rage.

She could not even stop to think what made him so angry. Her resistance and the strength probably arose from an unknown place inside when a soul refuses to be demeaned and then crushed.

He was obsessed and was going to conquer this little Yezidi girl. There was nothing or anyone near who was going to stop him. The other soldiers were in another part of the compound strategizing, eating and laughing.

Perhaps some or even entering the areas where other girls were staying. The women and children held captive were only a game to these pathetic warlords. They were preoccupied with money, murder and mayhem. This man, however, was preoccupied only with Nadja and stealing the innocence from her young body.

Nadja tried without success to find some place to go in her head that was filled with racing thoughts. She wanted to capture the essence of the distant memories that she had been blessed to explore just moments before this mad rapist entered her space.

She tried to settle her mind. He had stopped briefly and noticed that she was bloody and soiled from the previous beating that she had to take with the girls who had runaway.

They were lined up and beaten. She was also menstruating and there was nothing to stop her flow. He didn't care and acted as if this was the only time that he would be able to sneak in and molest her. She was merely inventory for the upcoming sex slave auction.

He demanded that she give him her undivided attention and give into his animal actions, or he would punish her in barbaric ways that she could not even imagine. His stare was a glimpse into hell. Nadja was consumed with fear. He smelled of urine mixed with sweat and her mind momentarily went back to her mother and what she had been forced to endure.

He had grabbed her by one leg and one arm pulling her down the hallway like a rag doll. She was tossed in a corner and her back violently hit the wall. He moved in and slapped her. He clawed at her clothing and ripped her dirty dress from her frail little body.

He saw that she was menstruating and for a brief moment he paused. Nadja thought that this would disgust him and that she would be left alone, but that would not be happening.

The man grabbed her by her hair, pulled her arms up over her head and bit her lips so she could not cry out. Then, because she was bleeding, he turned her around with full force pushed his way into her body, raping her from behind.

She felt a hot knife going in and out of her rectum and as he covered her mouth her muffled screams were to no avail. When he had finished with her he dropped her to the floor like so much trash....but she was still considered a virgin just in case she was chosen for "the sale".

The most frightening part of this tragic experience was that this beast was from another world. The two of them did not have language, manners or destiny in common.

It was all about power for him. He would not look into her eyes, nor relate to this child with any compassion concerning her future. He didn't care, and maybe even thought that he was doing her some kind of religious and male favor.

Her world was one of a peaceful existence and people simply did not assault people especially in lewd ways, even verbally. This man had no morals, not limits or boundaries.

He would probably be blown away by the bullets of the Peshmerga someday, at least she hoped so, and she would have to heal just from the contempt that she felt for someone she had been intimate with, but would never know. She knew that this attack would change her life forever and it did.

CHAPTER SIX

" MAYAN"

" We loved with a love that was more than love"
Edgar Allen Poe

It seemed that Nadja had already been in this compound for an eternity, when it was actually only months. One morning a new group of young women were brought to Raqqa to "pleasure" the militant soldiers.

Nadja felt horrible for them as she knew what they would all be subjected to. They had previously been at another location and their misery was going to be heightened to a new level. It was evident that all of these women had been severely beaten.

Their hands were tied in front of them and their faces were stained with the dirt of old tears. They all were very scared as they had no idea what awaited them at the new compound, but there were many of those whose eyes were glazed over as if they had already found a place in their psyche to retreat.

The situation had proven way too much for them to handle on a human level. There were many children brought in that had been previously sold. The little girls who were treated as human garbage and were thrown from the truck were amongst them.

Nadja was desperate to see who were the young girls in each group, because she was still looking for her little sister, Nasima. She had suddenly been separated from her mother and her little sister after the rape and then she was sold before their eyes. But, again to Nadja's despair she didn't appear in this group.

Then Nadja's heart broke inside her once again as she saw that some of the very youngest children already had fresh cigarette burns on their hands, arms and little legs. Nadja had watched from a dirty window as they brought each woman into the compound.

She had remembered the sad day she entered the filthy dungeon which was slow close to being in hell that she did not want to die and end up there. She watched them all being brutally pushed and dragged into the building.

Cattle were treated better with electric prods. This girls walked like the living dead, and didn't seem to care that they were being brought to a new place for new tortures. They were thin and barely alive, not just emaciated from the lack of food, but their lights were dim from the lack of being loved.

However, there was one girl who stood out amongst the captured girls. A girl who had been bought and sold. Nadja never thought that she would see this girl again in her wildest of dreams. Her name was Mayan, and of all people that Nadja had remembered, she did not believe that Mayan deserved these animals to even be near her.

Nadja knew what was in store for Mayan and she had also knew that her outcome would be hideous. Mayan was very beautiful. Mayan was from Nadja's Village of Sinjar, but they hadn't really known each other.

There were at least 100,000 people in the village, many of them related, and if they were not of the same family, everyone knew of each other's family and common heritage. Nadja had recognized Mayan right away as she walked slowly, and very broken from the truck, but then Nadja remembered the girl's former poise and beauty.

Mayan had been such a lovely girl, who had possessed such a fabulous love story. They had all believed that their story would be one of romance and interest for decades to come. Her inner and outer beauty was so evident that every girl in the village had envied her, along with her storybook marriage.

Nadja at that moment, could not believe her eyes and how old and frail Mayan had become. Nadja loved her and felt sorry for this young, broken princess. Nadja reached out to her and she and Mayan had become friends right away in Raqqa.

They had never thought in their wildest imagination that they would end up in circumstances like the ones in which they continued to suffer with what seemed as no way out.

One day, Mayan had been a young and beautiful bride in the village of Sinjar, dancing on a mountainside, and then in the twinkle of an eye, ends up a beaten and battered prisoner who was treated worse than any wild dog running on the mountain.

Mayan was just one year older then Nadja, but she became Nadja and the other girls' angel. She was so kind, and considerate regardless of the pitiful circumstances, and was always trying to keep the other girls in some kind of hopeful spirits.

This place compelled the young girls to create sort of a "sisterhood". This experience had created no illusion that they could go back to their homes and families. They could only endure the hideous tortures and think back each night that they had endured another day.

They got up every morning and slipped into the psychological bonds of ISIS for the sake of survival. Each girl was constantly on the "lookout" for loose weapons, forgotten pills and cell phones. Many times these were the keys to escape.

It was then that Nadja had discovered that she needed her new friend. Both her and Nadja had ended up without any family in Syria. They existed with strangers whose language and behaviors they did not understand, and whose demonic nightly actions were beyond anything they could mentally and emotionally comprehend. There was no language for this.

Nadja had always looked up to Mayan from afar, and now she had become a prisoner like herself. Yet, neither of them could allow themselves to dwell on the past for fear of having a complete breakdown. Yet, sometimes old memories brought strength. Strength to believe in God, themselves and life in some aspect of the future.

Hope was still springing in Nadja's broken heart. She held onto Mayan's words as she recanted their beautiful wedding story. Mayan sobbed as she spoke, as well could be expected when she mentioned her love and memories of Salaam.

Absolutely everyone who was Yezidi had heard about Mayan and Salaam's love. It was legendary. These were two young people who were really committed to each other. Their friends had never stopped talking about their precious relationship.

Mayan had only been with her new husband, Salaam for six months, when ISIS showed up to kill and capture those living in Sinjar. She could not believe that they would be forever be apart now. She had grown to depend on him as her best friend. He was such a part of her being and she did not realize how much until he was gone.

Some people even wrote songs about those two as if they were some kind of folk heroes. Their romance became the talk of the village. Salaam had loved her with a burning passion and he would end up proving his total and complete dedication with his life.

In Yezidi tradition young girls married so very young and it was a mystery how they knew what their hearts were saying so clearly immediately.

It is strange how even the very young know that marriage is an eternal sacrament and were well aware of the responsibilities that went along with that love. Each person must marry within the Yezidi community; there are also restrictions on marriages between the clerical and lay classes and between relatives.

Love is the basis in which Yezidi partners choose each other and not previous arrangements such as in other cultures. However, this mutual attraction, and intent to marry must still be through and by the consent of their respective family heads.

Divorce is rare but can be obtained, however the testimony of witnesses to infidelity is sometimes necessary. Also, if a Yezidi man were to leave the community and remain abroad for more than a year, his marriage can be annulled. He may also be forbidden to marry another Yezidi woman as well.

Polygamy was allowed for men, and there was no limit on the number or frequency of marriages per man. A woman could not marry multiple men, however.

It is still considered necessary for each family to agree to the prospective union and neither family could find it in their heart to do so.

A poor man, or a non-relative, would often choose this route of stealing his bride, if he felt the woman's father would not allow the marriage. Close relatives within the Faqier caste, even first cousins, were preferred spouses generally.

An interesting note is that in Armenia where a large population of the Yezedis have fled, Yezidis generally do not marry outside their class —and never marry Kurds. Some assimilated urban Yezidis have married Armenians. The class system was more lenient.

But in Sinjar their was no exceptions. Their rules required a dowry to be paid to the bride's family, negotiated between the families. A man could steal an unmarried woman, flee to a relative's house, and at the same time gain consent to marry with payment of a bride price.

There were two castes in the Yezedi Community and Mayan belonged to the family that was the most highly regarded and definitely of the highest order of the Yezedis.

Mayan was from the tier that provided the direction and all of the leaders and elders to the community as a whole. Theirs was a highly prestigious position and family as far as the Yezidis are concerned.

Love in the Yezidi community comes with a high price, literally. A man can only have one wife, and he desired no one but Mayan. This is the rule, except for wealthy or high-ranking individuals (e.g., the emir, who may take six or more wives).

Mayan's family would ask for the maximum price because of their position in the village. Salaam was just a poor shepherd and did not know that he had to pay an exorbitant bride-price (kalam) for Mayan. This was to be only paid in gold to the woman's father or brother, and they demanded some money along with the gold.

Elopements are quite common, where the groom kidnaps his bride and then pays for her later at a big wedding party celebration. These events are sometimes secretly arranged by the couple to avoid such major expense, but neither one of these two lovers wanted to disappoint their parents.

This would not be considered to be a stoning offense for the woman, or a cause for banishment of the man. Rather, it would be considered a sign of the man's strength. But, Salaam would not hear of anyone but Mayan and present her as the most beloved bride that were ever married in the Yezidi Community.

They wanted the world to see and be a part of their vows on a special day. But it was apparent that these two lovers would be inseparable. Their love would last through the ages as they fought even to marry and would not succumb to family pressures of different classes marrying.

It was obvious that they were going to go ahead with their wedding plans or they would have no choice but to elope. The parents of Salaam did not have the money to pay for his intended bride. There were rules for the rituals.

They had told their mothers of their mutual pledge in confidence, but without telling their fathers. Mothers in the most communities are far more romantic and sympathetic to young love. After all, they were once young and had over heels with the father of their children.

Mayan and Salaam pulled on the hearts of their mothers. They threatened to either elope, or approach their fathers, make an agreement between the families, and announce the wedding, but they didn't know which.

Then before they could decide, her grandfather suddenly died. According to custom, they had to wait one year for the usual grieving period before they could marry, with monthly memorial lunches in her grandfather's honor.

The two would have to wait a year, but they could not show disrespect to his family by violating the grieving period. They had a large lunch for mourners on each of five successive days in a big tent erected for the purpose on the street in front of their house.

This couple had remembered their first meeting so well. Mayan wasn't shy about showing that she had already fallen in love with him from a distance and she had trusted her instincts fully. It was not blind love. She had already sensed his gentle manner, his honesty, his conservative movements, and his easy but modest smile. Those were markers for other good traits that she knew she could trust. His words, lack of money, or his family were not of great concern to her by then.

The matter would be proven in time, and this gave them the chance to explore a friendship over time. The intensity of this first meeting was great, and the ten minutes seemed a hundred.

They didn't dare to talk longer, as it would have tipped others off to their mutual pledge too early, before they could savor the precious moment privately to themselves, sabotaging their chances for additional conversations before the pressure from friends entered the picture.

Salaam was beside himself with happiness at her acceptance. Mayan felt a great comfort and release, as the pressures on her to marry were already great, with Yezidi girls being allowed to marry as young as ten, and many were marrying when they were thirteen or fourteen.

Both Salaam and Mayan were more sensible than most, and they would allow time for their relationship to build from their initial feelings to something more substantial that could sustain them through the years. Still, it had to be made clear that the interest was in marriage from the beginning, or all the conversations afterward would not have been acceptable.

He had told his best friend Ziad and she told her best friend Jihan. Telling another person made it more real, more legitimate, and allowed them to share the weight of their excitement. In the next few months they found many opportunities to meet at various wedding parties and festivals.

He secretly bought a telephone for her so they could talk more often. She hid the phone so her family wouldn't discover it. It was not formally accepted for girls to talk on phones to boys, but it was becoming common practice.

They usually talked late at night, often for an hour or two. They always chose public venues for meetings arranged by telephone. Sometimes they exchanged little gifts.

First, he had given her some beautiful flowers from the fields. She cherished these and placed them between two pieces of paper to keep them for all eternity, as far as she was concerned. She then in turn made and gave him a simple red, tiny stringed necklace.

The red and white threads were interwoven. It was a simple and not only identified him as an Yezidi young man, but this was given as a gift as was the custom for the Yezidi New Year, on the first Wednesday in April.

Their families were not aware of their friendship for a year, after which time others began to see them together and talking and smiling at parties. Soon everyone caught on that these two were deeply in love.

People not only noticed but told their respective mothers. Both mothers were supportive, and considered a prospective marriage, although Salaam never told his father. Matchmaking was the business of mothers in the early stages, with fathers stepping in for the final agreements.

The Yezidis live in nuclear-family groups. The father is head of the household and exercises full authority over his wife and children. Salaam was the eldest son and was second in authority in his family's home. But, Salaam's family was from the second class.

The order that was common. Salaam's parents were poor. They had no educational training or responsibilities in the village. They could not afford to risk a blood feud over a girl in the village or risk being excommunicated for not complying to strict moral codes.

This was to lead to one of the most controversial relationships that the village had ever known. All of the elders and other leaders who are in higher esteem were called upon to try to talk to the young people about their future association. Each family was in agreement about the only one thing—that these two should call off their love, and stop any future contact, but these two would have not of it.

His parents had known that this love affair was going to turn out to be a preverbal war within the village. They had begged Salaam not to involve himself with Mayan. They were wrought with distress as they knew that these two young lovers were at the mercy of the decision of the elders of the village.

But the village was happy for Mayan. She had found love. Everyone who knew Mayan's family came and paid their respects. The ritual was well established. Old and middle aged, Faqier Yezidi men sat on floor cushions around the walls and in the middle of the room facing both sides.

Water was poured over their hands into a plastic basin by the younger men. Salaam and his brother Faisal were among them, and towels were shared for drying.

Large stainless steel platters of rice, cous-cous, with chicken and lamb on top, and large flat disks of homemade bread were brought in. Salads were laid before them, with olives, onions, tomato, cucumbers and herbs.

Meat and juice was poured over the rice and cous-cous so to allow it to stick together when they pinched it with their fingers. The women remained out of sight, preparing the food and cleaning up afterward, sometimes stopping to talk and cry together.

Then it happened. After the grieving period and several meetings between the parents and the elders of the community, they were miraculously given permission to wed.

It was truly an historical miracle. It virtually stood as a decision and an agreement that had rarely been made between these classes. Salaam and Mayan had convinced their parents and the community leaders that they needed to be together forever.

This was pretty much unheard of and marked a historic turning point in centuries of religious and family rituals. They were the talk of the Yezidi community all the way to Armenia. Their love had conquered the normal traditions.

Salaam's family arranged to pay 3,500,000 Iraqi Dinars ($2,931USD) to her family, and bought 75 grams of gold jewelry, worth 1,500,000 Iraqi Dinars ($1,256USD), as part of her bride price.

Her family would lose any benefit from her labor, and the gold was both an honor to her and financial security for her and their children in a land that often claims the lives of young husbands and fathers early. It was the same price Islamic terrorists nearby charged for young Yezidi women of her age and beauty, and also the price of an great horse.

Publicly they were ready to declare their love. Their wedding was spectacular as weddings go in the village. It was a fabulous celebration and no one wanted to miss it.

The whole village came out and attended the celebration with cheers and shouts. Mayan and Salaam we're celebrated like Yezidi royalty. Even the bride's family began to rejoice with them, and little did they know this would be the last wedding that their family would ever participate in.

Salaam's family was just as excited as they should've been because his bride was the most beautiful girl in the village. Salaam was the envy of every Yezidi young man for miles around.

Their marriage ceremony began with the family escorting her from her father's house to that of Salaam. Along the way she prayed at every shrine she encountered, including the Christian churches. When she arrived at the Salaam's home, he greeted her with a blow from a small stone, to indicate her submission to him from then on.

As a bride she remained in the Salaam's house for three days, concealed behind a curtain in a darkened room, during which time he could not see her. On the evening of the third day the sheikh solemnized the marriage in a brief ceremony, marked by the bride and groom each taking the end of a stick and breaking it, to symbolize the intactness of their relationship until death breaks it asunder.

Mayan was radiant as she was dressed in the most beautiful white wedding dress. It was handmade, but more elegant than any thing purchased in a store filled with gowns. Her hair was pulled back and laid softly upon her head, revealing the extra makeup that every bride adorned herself with in Sinjar.

She had dark painted eyes, but the shadows only brought out the beauty of the two pools of love she had for Salaam. She wore a beautiful red lace sash around her waist that made her look particularly thin.

This sash had been worn by Yezidi brides for centuries declaring not only their love for their groom, but a love for their people as well. She carried a beautiful bouquet of fresh flowers, and she beamed with joy as she stood next to Salaam.

Her groom stood by her dressed in a beautiful black suit and crisp white shirt. He too wore red with a tie that was as bright and luscious as her lips. Even his eyes smiled. He was filled with joy and his chest stuck out with the pride that only a groom who has chosen his new wife for life could exhibit. They were and exquisite couple.

Their love was made in Heaven and even hell could not separate their hearts, when it would soon rear its ugly head. Mayan and Salaam were prominently featured, sitting on separate chairs, with several bouquets of flowers placed in front of them.

Guests paraded by them, especially the middle-aged women and older girls, while men generally watched from a distance, with economy of movement and speech directed toward one another more than to the couple or their close family members. Music played loudly in the background and rose to fill the village and the mountain beyond with the celebration.

Then the dancing began and the people rejoiced with them. They danced and laughed the afternoon and early night away. Each person bestowed wonderful gifts on them, and lavished so much gold and money upon this couple, even by Salaam's family, that it amazed both families. They were so loved that the price that had to be paid for Mayan was met and exceeded.

When the dance music grew loudest the people brought them necklaces, pins, earrings, and rings, all made of gold, and pressed money into the folds of their clothing to great applause. This indicated to them that they were blessed and that they should be together in their love without any regrets.

When one left the table, another took his place, until all had their fill of the delicious food and tea, men with men, women with women. Boys cleaned up the abundance of left-overs to be distributed among their neighbors and friends.

The tables were cleaned, folded, and set to the side. Boys used the occasion to strut around in their finest clothes, exploring the way the clothes moved against their clean bodies and growing muscles and propping up the longer strands of their short, heavily gelled hair on the crowns of their heads to maximum height.

Girls swayed about in groups of two to four, in shimmering fabrics that flowed as they moved, capturing bits of sunlight on sequins and gold colored threads, their long hair draped over their shoulders. Older boys briefly met girls they fancied, small children ran about playing chase, and older men and women sought benches or small carpets in groups to talk as it pleased them.

Then they were finally alone for the first time after what seemed an eternity of waiting. They walked together, arm in arm, into the little Temple. Their feet stopped there, but their hearts didn't.

First they thanked God for bringing them together, with their eyes closed, their hands held gently. Their first kiss was a tender one, saved for that special moment. Salaam held her closely to affirm that there would never again be space between them.

Mayan melted in the embrace of his arms, and knew she was finally home. Nothing else mattered. And it would only be in death that they would be torn apart physically, but her feelings still remained for Salaam, as if it were the first day they knew that they were destined to be together forever.

After dinner, the young adults and some of the middle-aged family members danced together upon the mountain for several hours until sunset, holding hands with their elbows bent, their feet stepping slowly sideways, knees bending and shoulders shaking in a complicated rhythmic sequence to centuries-old florid music belted out in solos by young men and boys that had been prerecorded and played by a DJ.

The singing was accompanied by the stringed tamboor, played horizontally with a pick against the steady beat of the sheepskin dulzerna. It grew somewhat louder as the pace of the music and the height of the dance stepping increased, reaching a crescendo at the late evening hour of eleven. Mayan was the center of attention of all the people dancing or looking on with joy. She stepped lightly in her beautiful dress, smiled brightly, and basked in the admiration she saw in Salaam's light brown eyes.

Salaam had given great thought to his life. Working and caring for the sheep had given him hours every day to think about his life, present, past and future. They were essentially the same thoughts from the day before, and the day before that, with few changes, but they were his.

They were similar to the thoughts of a thousand shepherds before him in the same field at the base of the same mountain. He was not much troubled by the outside world until it appeared in his village in some way that was threatening to his family.

Some shepherds used their idle days to hone their shooting skills, rock-throwing skills, or wood-carving skills, or carried along friends to add drama and counter-play.

Salaam used the time to absorb the colored light cast by the rocks, grass, brush, and even the sheep, contemplate their colors, watch them change, and to relive past moments in his mind.

In the past six months, the moments with his new wife were filling his thoughts: her tender looks, the warmth of her body against his, and her words and expressions of every kind. He had found her as varied as the colors on the landscape before him. His body ached to be with her again by mid-afternoon.

The time to leave the fields in the later afternoon was chosen by the sheep, not by his own desires or inclinations, or even by the time or the position of the sun.

The dominant ram influenced the timing more than he did, keenly sensing the mood of the ewes and younger, older, and smaller rams, which varied by the abundance of food in the fields.

Salaam honored the role of the ram, and left him to do his work. But even with the decision made, and announced by the ram's own voice, Salaam was still needed to be herdsman, and to use his voice and position to guide the strays.

The herd was small enough that he did not cultivate the assistance of a sheep dog, but this meant he had to be more active and more vocal in moving among the sheep.

The grass was abundant, so the donkey that accompanied him on the journey, and hovered among the sheep during the day, was more a companion than a means of transportation, except in cases of emergency, or a way to carry a wounded or sick sheep home.

The sheep filed directly back into their home shelter and took a drink of water before bedding down for the evening.

Salaam secured the door of the enclosure, entered the gate to his uncle's garden, said goodbye to those gathered in the garden, and headed home.

He entered his own garden and greeted his brother Faisal and sister Basse. His eyes gauged their mood carefully as he moved through the garden toward the house, giving each one, in turn, a kiss on the cheek of equal affection and magnitude.

His siblings welcomed the scheduled rarity of Salaam's appearance from the fields as a relief from the directives of their parents and grandmother who checked them throughout mid-day.

There were sometimes petty arguments between them all, but Salaam was the wise, gentle, arbitrator appearing after all cases were stated between opposing parties. If they were presented in his absence he would always make it a point to settle matters of the day upon his return with a simple word or two.

It was the sound of his words, spoken in the deep clear musical tones of young manhood, more than their meaning, that calmed and comforted them.

He moved through the family members in the garden as if parting great waters, bent on reaching the other side to the ready arms of Mayan.

Each family member adored her as much as he did, but there were few displays of affection between husband and wife under the watchfulness of the family. And they were watching intently.

Salaam would continue to steal a glance, however, and Mayan would melt at his gaze. They were young, in love and hadn't a care in the world.

Intimate moments were finally stolen in their locked room beside a water-cooled fan in the late summer afternoon. There secret place was where they shared kisses and sweet words rather than on the roof at night.

There were only small distances that separated the two couples, the grandmother and his sister, and his brother, in respective corners of the roof. They all retreated to the roof for a little comfort. The house was too hot for sleeping on summer nights.

Their intimate moments were more precious due to their limited frequency. The afternoon's rest in their private shaded room was a blessed antidote to the searing heat of the fields for Salaam, and for Mayan, a relief from the occasional perceived slight of her female in-laws. They relished their private time together.

They separately disappeared into the room after she finished her chores and after he washed the dust of the fields from his face and hands. He entered first, and stretched out on a foam mat on the bare concrete floor, then she joined him there.

He held her tenderly, closely, for a while, then kissed her on her lean white cheek and forehead, then on her soft red lips. She responded to him in kind, following his lead.

Then they held one another for more than an hour, first talking of the events of her day, her concerns about the future and the baby, their hopes of a home of their own one day.

They spoke to each other about their concerns about the Daesh terrorists encroaching on the region, before falling asleep in one another's arms. The swamp cooler in the window blew damp, cooler air over them and they laughed and imagined felt like an ocean breeze.

Salaam and Mayan had lived in what was perceived poverty for several reasons. Living near the mountain meant a rural life on poor lands left to a people shunted aside by the dominant cultures for their religious beliefs. Living close to the mountain had always been their way to survive genocide.

The Yezidi caste system had placed them on the bottom tier of society. Mayan lived with Salaam's poor family and didn't mind as she loved Salaam with all of her heart and soul.

Rising above these "written in stone "conditions, in the short term to enjoy a better life would require leaving their village, their culture, their religion, and probably their country.

Even if they were willing to do that, they would find it nearly impossible to gather enough money to escape. They also knew even in a western country, as immigrants not knowing the language, they would find themselves in abject poverty, working low-skilled jobs at least in the beginning.

They would have to hold off on any immediate plans to change their future outlook. The were content, however, with each other and related like they had been married for decades.

The news also came quickly to the couple that they were expecting a baby. They were poor and could now barely make ends meet, but that did not hamper their joy!

Their sense of family responsibility, and Mayan's pregnancy, prevented them even from seriously considering escape from Iraq, though others often discussed it and told stories of those who had escaped.

Salaam and Mayan carried this knowledge heavily as they thought of bringing a new child into the world. They were determined not to convert to the Muslim religion, no matter what the cost, a determination that had grown solid as a rock within their people over time.

Their short rest that afternoon left them comforted in one another's presence, yet troubled in heart at the prospects for their future. Salaam emerged first from their room in the evening to heat the water and wash for dinner, and Mayan followed soon after.

She would be helping Salaam's married sister Gule, his mother Kamela, and his grandmother Shereen prepare the dinner. It would be a typical dinner of cucumber, hot beans and rice, with a little meat.

By the time the dishes were washed and the food put away Zere had returned to her husband's family's house, Salaam's father had said the evening prayers on the roof facing the sunset, the sun had already fallen, and the others were settled into their beds and slowly moving and talking less and falling asleep. Thoughts of the future would cease with with the settling sun.

SALAAM

Salaam had joined his father on the rooftop looking to the West and seeing the last glimmers of light across the Iraqi border with Syria. "Father, do you have enough ammunition to carry with you tonight?" he asked.

His father would regularly take that duty required of one member of each family for ten day intervals on and off, leaving Salaam free to get some sleep at night and herd the sheep during the day.

Then his father would return in the morning and sleep through till the afternoon before going to work laying concrete blocks when there was work. "The little I have would not last long if we were assaulted, but I will use it carefully," he replied.

"Should we ask Khudeda to buy some more when he goes to Duhok next time?" Salaam asked. "No," he answered, "we need to save our money to buy food."

Salaam left it at that, and a long pause came in their conversation as they both silently contemplated the likely situation of his father being stuck defending the village in a Daesh (ISIS) invasion and running out of ammunition.

They had no specific plan about how long he would stay on the front line after an attack, whether they would wait for him to flee to the mountain, and what they would carry.

"Well, goodnight," Salaam finally said, and he walked across the roof to join his wife, who was laying out their bed. Salaam changed his clothes and laid down beside her. His father left soon after for his duty with the militia, but Salaam didn't hear him go.

The night was quiet, as always, the electric services were both off for the night. The whole village was dark, and nearly all who were not guarding the village were in their beds or on their way to them.

Salaam prayed what was in his heart, not a memorized prayer, then laid down and took Mayan into his arms, her head upon his chest, his mind unsettled but tired of body, and he quickly fell off to sleep.

Then, a single gunshot suddenly broke the silence and ended her future dreams. Salaam knew the sound of a bullet discharged from a Russian Kalashnakov rifle. It was an old rifle with a distinct sound. It was as familiar to him as the crow of his rooster at sunrise.

Their four eyes opened instantly, mechanically, as if connected to the lever action of the rifle's trigger, and quickly met for reassurance. "Must have been a misfire from one of the men guarding the village," he offered quietly to calm her, seeing the fear cut lines into in her face.

She said nothing, but nestled closer to him, finding safety in his arms as they closed tightly around her. As she held her abdomen with this precious gift of life that filled her she knew that this was the beginning of the end of their joy. These fond memories from six months before were still playing out in Mayan's dreams as she lay sleeping on the roof in his arms in the early morning hours on August 3rd, 2014.

Meanwhile, Salaam's father walked down the road in the darkness toward the checkpoint by the line of men standing guard over the village.

He said "Choani, Bashi?" meaning "How are you, well?" in his native Kurmanji Kurdish to his several cousins and other friends as they drank morning tea at the base of a mound of dirt that had been dozed there in a long line to shield them from possible invaders.

One man was silently checking in with the father's unspoken expressions as he felt a certain level of distress. They just knew that things were escalating to a point that there was no return. ISIS would be swift and determined to take the village regardless of age or gender, every person would be subjugated to a horrible outcome.

From the roof, still watching for his father, Salaam saw families running to them from Jazeera and Guzarik villages on either side of Tel Azer, with blood on their faces, warning them to leave. Their weak mud brick, mud mortared houses had collapsed on top of them when shelled by Daesh, wounding many and killing some.

Meanwhile Salaam's mother Kamela, grandmother Shereen, and sister Basse gathered the most important things, taking photos out of albums so they would be lighter to carry, checking to see that all their IDs were together.

They took all of their money from its hiding place, and choosing carefully what little food and water they would carry, and what vessels or bags they would use to carry it. They chose only the most essential clothes to carry with them.

Two of Shereen's sons, Salaam's uncles, arrived to carry her in their car to the mountain, where Salaam's family arranged to meet them at Qandil. Salaam's family had no car or other vehicle to transport them, so they would have to walk all the way to the mountain. There was no room for them in the car Salaam's uncles had just bought.

Shereen was 70, and extremely frail, which made it was necessary for Salaam to help her. He could see people in the village carrying their elderly and disabled in wheelbarrows or on their backs, but he felt this would be too jarring for his elderly grandmother.

Some were leaving their elderly and sick behind as they were unable to walk or weak enough that they chose to take their chances with the Peshmerga and militia. In Salaam's family, however, Shereen was given first priority for evacuation. She was a matriarch's matriarch and they would care for her with their lives.

This time was all together different and they all knew it. Lives were depending upon their swift flight. There had been many threats on the lives and the total culture of the Yezidis. This time however there was a brutal and evil nemesis lurking who had shown no mercy as they made their way across Iraq.

There was no time to assess any part of the situation. Leave everything that was dear behind, and hope that there was some rescue operation up ahead.

However, it was confirmed that ISIS was on the way. The only thing that they could try to do was make it to the mountains. They quickly distributed the items prepared for carrying.

Shereen was picked up by two of her sons with their families, but there was no room for the others. Cousins and close friends were just going t have to make a run for it. Salaam and his parents carried clothes, food, and water, and his father carried his Kalashnikov weapon just in case he could get bullets somewhere.

Within a few minutes, they were on their way walking as quickly as they could toward the mountain in a scene of ultimate terror, a mix of people and animals running in every direction on foot and in trying to load up and flee in vehicles. In that moment, as they left their house, they were taking a big step deeper into poverty.

The house they left behind was their own, though it was not much. They would have no means to get another. The loss of the sheep would leave them with no source of milk, meat and yoghurt or cash from the hides. There would be no bread oven, no household items for cooking, no beds and blankets for sleeping, and no extra clothes.

Years would pass without them seeing their house and village again, if ever. They and the people who had visited their home frequently would be psychologically traumatized.

Many, including some they loved, would be killed, wounded, or captured and raped repeatedly by their captors in the name of an extremist form of Islam. It was a dark hour, the darkest most of them would ever know, though many dark days were yet ahead of them.

Both men were aware that Islamic terrorists from ISIS were threatening to invade from their nearby stronghold of Mosul, a satellite of their headquarters in Raqqa, Syria.

Then his father's other close friend called three hours later on the telephone to say that Daesh, who is ISIS, was entering Tel Azer. Salaam rushed to the other side of the house and saw Daesh invading with 50 trucks from two directions, trying to circle the people to prevent them from fleeing to Mount Sinjar.

They were distinguishable by their all-black clothing, U.S. army and Saudi Arabian vehicles, and black flags with white Arabic words proclaiming that they were the army of God.

As they approached, they were shooting every man they encountered, and every child who ran away, and capturing the women and children who didn't run away to put on a bus for sale as sex slaves or to hold for ransom.

They had busses and excavation machines waiting behind their force for the swift processing and relocation of female slaves and their children and for the mass burials of men, older boys, and many of the the elderly and disabled.

Salaam's family hid inside their house and bolted the door. It was 7:30 am when his father arrived from the front lines, covered in dirt, and called through the locked door. They opened the door to him together, and threw their arms around him. He had been spared.

"The front lines have been breached and I think most of the Kurds left before I did," he said. "I ran out of bullets, and the others had little to spare," he said, more to calm his own feelings of having abandoned the field than to calm theirs.

Some of the local men are still fighting there but they won't be able to hold out much longer." A man of 66 did not need to excuse himself for having fought terrorists on the front line for a shorter time than younger men. He was an exceptional man, and held himself and his children to high standards.

Salaam had tried to escape with his family and it was a last ditch effort to make it to freedom. He grabbed Mayan and his grandmother that was so dear to him. But this was to no avail.

He ran as far as he could and then ISIS shined their lights on a young man whom they considered a threat. Mayan was pulled away from Salaam screaming and holding her abdomen.

She didn't know if she had pains from the baby inside of her or from the brutal treatment that was being inflicted on the love of her life. It was all too much for her.

They circled him and then Mayan saw Salaam beaten with the butt of a rifle, his skull crushed on one side, and then the ISIS soldier laughed, shot him first in both of his knees, then in his shoulders, and finally in the head twice.

Mayan fainted, but someone had taken the stringed necklace from Salaam's bloody neck, and when she had finally woke up in a semi-conscious blur, she felt the string. Someone had placed it in her hand. She was screaming from her heart, and the people who were left in the village heard her painful shriek. They were as helpless as Mayan.

SWEET DEATH

Mayan had been in the initial sweep that had killed so many, wounded more and captured the souls of the women who had been in the right place at the wrong time. She had viewed the plundering of lives and families as the bus pulled away. No one had escaped the onslaught. Men lie dead in all the village roads, eyes staring upward.

She had forced herself to look out of the window regardless of the pillaging to take a final look at her home. She tired to remember just one moment of joy, but ISIS had stolen all of that away.

She felt the bumps beneath the tires and wondered whose family members we're being crushed. She would never forget the horrible feeling of knowing that loved ones had been so easily discarded.

Mayan stared out the window to try to see Salaam's body, but she could not make out a single man on a pile. It was a surreal scene as bodies who were alive just the day before were meshed together in death.

They had no identity, no smiles, no color, just masses of human flesh that would leave this world without dignity or grace. They looked strange in death. Like people that she had never known.

She had just wanted to kiss his cold lips and say goodbye just one more time. This would prove to be impossible as the huge machine had already scooped up his body and dumped him in a mass grave like so much debris.

She was sickened by this thought, but it had been better to not see flies light on him with the morning light coming. Her family was already gone and she was sure that most of the men had been slaughtered.

The bus had driven on and Mayan had lost all hope until she encountered some of the girls from the village in the one the other compounds for sex slaves that they had been taken. They were almost lifeless, but still familiar to Mayan. They were now all sisters in this horrible situation. Most had been sold over and over again.

Mayan had been sold to many owners in a few months, but she was never mistreated or abused. But now she was seeing the picture of her captivity from a different angle. She needed someone to explain how this new compound was run. She needed a good friend and fast.

Nadja was to be one of the best friends that she would ever encounter. They held each other and cried. Nadja tried to comfort her upon hearing the story. She could relate now on so many levels, except the about being in love. That was stolen from her in the dead of the night by thieves who enjoyed the pain and suffering.

Everyone in the village knew of Mayan and Salaam's love and sacrifice for each other. She could not nor did she have to explain the heartache of losing her love. Mayan was frantic but exhausted. She fell asleep in Nadja's arms.

It didn't matter that Mayan was pregnant. The ISIS soldiers at the present compound had spotted this beauty right away. They were not so secretly fighting over which one would have at her first. This went on for several days, and just when she thought that they would not resolve their sick claims, things took a turn for the worst.

Although, Mayan was instructed by Nadja not to bathe, because then she would be considered more undesirable, this did not stop the soldiers from looking at her and talking amongst themselves.

They were up to something but Mayan did not know what exactly. Mayan had even tried to explain to the soldier that brought them a biscuit and a little water that she was pregnant. He just turned, laughed and then walked away.

Then in the middle of the same night she was awakened from a light sleep and brought to another area of the compound. She kept trying to explain that she was already pregnant, and although she pleaded for them to show compassion they refused to believe her. They slapped her for lying and lectured her in Arabic about the sin of lying.

Her clothes were ripped from her body. They pushed her from man to man and each one would deliberately touch her in such a vile way that she finally just fell to the floor weeping. They were angry that she had retreated to the floor. This only caused them to be more aggressive.

She was picked up by one of the men and slammed into a filthy pile of old sheets. They were stained with old body fluids and blood. She turned her head to one side and vomited. She was pulled out of her vomit, flipped to the other end of the bed.

They did not even bother to take the sheets filled with vomit from the pile. Two of the men held her her down. They grabbed her legs and arms like human vice grips.

Other men then brought water turned her head to the side and several pills were forced into her mouth. These were a combination of sleeping pills and birth control pills.

Mayan was an 18-year-old Yezidi girl who had committed no crime except that she was beautiful. Her glow was from being loved and carrying the child of a man who adored her.

The militants took turns raping her. She kept fading in and out of consciousness, but when she would slightly come to, she was seeing different faces at different moments.

They were using her body like a rag doll. She was turned, propped and rolled over for men to take advantage of her for hours. Some took several turns. She thought that she was watching and not in a nightmare.

She grappled with her own mind to wake up. She was in a bad dream that was surreal and one that she could not awaken from. It was real. Her worst fears had been realized. The numerous men kept up the assault for most of the night.

Yet, just when this young woman didn't think that things were to get any worse it happened. She saw lights flashing but she had no idea of what these animals had intended. She was incoherent for the most part, but still with her body writhing in pain involuntarily, she could see them huddled around her and hear their voices.

She saw men pushing to get in line. This meant that the ordeal would continue and continue. She finally went unconscious for the final moments of the ordeal. She passed out into oblivion and could dream about nothing else except Salaam and their families.

She was aware of her surroundings, but the pills had somewhat softened the hellish blow. She could not track the sequence of her attack. She was thankful that she missed most of the onslaught. They had her body but they didn't have her mind.

When all the men had left the room, they had several of the girls come and take her off the bed and carry her battered body down the hallway.

She tried to take steps herself to show the militants that they had not conquered her souls. With two steps out of the room, she collapsed immediately. The baby was born and died on the cold floor of the compound.

She had pleaded with them at first telling them that she was pregnant. They laughed and handed her body one to the other like meat in storage locker. She was too weak to deal with the tragedy of losing her family, her husband, her body and her baby all in a few short days.

She was laid down in another room to try and recover but this was to no avail. She was bleeding profusely and she had loss the use of her legs, even if it was to be temporary. She didn't know or care.

Then, the militants came back to take her again. She could not physically withstand anymore of their animal sadism. They proceeded to drag her down the hall and sat her in a chair.

There they were laughing and talking amongst themselves. They pointed at her and then dimmed the lights. Now she remembered and understood the flashes.

They had video taped the whole dark event. She was forced to watch and she felt her life leave her body. She did not want to live another day. They had not tortured her enough, but then began to beat her and tell her in Arabic that she was now a Muslim. She spit on the floor and one of them slapped her unconscious.

Nadja knew that it was just a matter of time before Mayan joined Salaam and their baby. She was right as only one week passed before Mayan had joined many other girls in killing herself with a pistol that she had found.

The militants were found crying as they were insisting that she had no right to rob them of their religious pleasures. With this one shot she had flown from their grasp…by her own hand with dignity and confidence in Salaam meeting her in the clouds.

CHAPTER SEVEN
"ESCAPE"

" Courage is grace under pressure"
Earnest Hemingway

Nadja's world had immediately expanded. She was taken from the only home that she had ever known and was brought in and treated as less than human in an even even stranger environment.

Nadja had not been sold, but was a sex slave for the compound. She had been passed around like a well worn garment. She didn't know what was worse, living with some strange family in another country, or being subjected to the ongoing tortures of the hellish nights for almost a year.

The options ran equal in Nadja's mind. Nadja lay in her makeshift bed with her thoughts running wild. For the very first time in her life she was experiencing a new emotion. She had nothing to be angry about in Sinjar, except the occasional disagreement about her home chores.

Maybe, she had gone a little overboard when her siblings didn't listen and had gone to the fields to play instead of clean or peel the potatoes. She had always found them and scolded when they did not carry out their mother's wishes.

Their father was seldom at home and her mom had needed all hands on deck to keep the house running smoothly. Nadja had daily fought the battle between loving the outdoors, going to school, being with her friends from the village, and home.

She cherished her independence, and when walking up the mountain, her imagination ran wild. She loved her freedom, however, she always glad to help. The children would all finally comply and always give in when it came to their mother's requests.

This time she would not cooperate. She would not allow herself to be a casualty, but she would use her rage for something far more productive. Her anger was fueled as she couldn't help but feel the pains in her body and remember the agonizing screams and moans from the the other girls.

The nights had become far to long and she would see the sun rise from the mountains again or die trying. The anger in her heart had grown like a cancer. She cried herself to sleep when ISIS wasn't using her body like a rag, wiping off their murderous exploits.

They went from village to village foraging and pillaging the name of their so-called religion. No one could identify any of the tenants that they so profusely swore by, but they were certain that every man, woman, and child should be forced to join their order.

Something surprising had risen up in Nadja. She had been taught by the best to never give up. Rooba was not only her mother but her best friend on Earth. Rooba did not let them win and neither would Nadja. She could hear her mother's sweet voice whisper to her from some eternal canyon.

It seemed to say, "Nadja, LIVE". Nadja had stopped teaching for answers and now decided deep within the realms of her non existence that she did not want her mother and father's deaths to be in vain.

But something had to shift in Nadja. She would have to move, and she would have to dispense of the heartaches and fear that kept her immobile. These men were not infallible, and their only motivation was to hurt others. They were perverted in every aspect and this, Nadja thought, would soon have them off their guard.

Nadja had begun to reminisce. This gave her She remembered that day even more clearly now. It had been such a hot, sweltering morning in August over one year ago. No one had really slept the night before. Every family was in sheer panic .

Their therapy to try and face the harsh reality was to hurry and attempt to pack up the remains of their shattered lives. Clothing, pictures and jewelry that they would never need again.

She could still hear the sound of her mother, Rooba's voice asking her to help her get things ready around the house when company was coming over.

Her father had been cut to pieces by a stream of bullets right in front of her eyes. He had not trial, no jury, no defense…just judgement and execution for being Yezidi.

Did it take that much gunfire to kill one innocent, unarmed man, she wondered? He had left his guns behind in a hurry to try to get his family to safety.

His rifles would not have helped because he was surrounded by so many cowards. They filled their bellies with satisfaction as they murdered the helpless.

Their father seemed to always be having a conversation with the neighborhood men about new businesses and politics in Kurdistan. Nadja would give anything to help her mother in the kitchen, and to hear those voices again once more.

Yet, she knew that she would not hear those beloved sounds again. ISIS had seen to that. could have thrown her body in front of his, she would have been honored.

The most painful part of that ordeal was in the fact that his eyes had pierced her heart as he fell to the ground on that fateful day. His eyes seemed to say, "take good care of your mother."

By all accounts of that final commission she had failed miserably. She had not been allowed to run to him to hold his head in her arms and neither was her mother. And Rooba was nw gone.

His body released his soul to the wind. In a moment his life had ceased, and everything moved so swiftly that her father was not even given the privilege of one final struggle. Nadja rested in the knowledge that her father was much braver than what ISIS had allowed him to appear to be.

Nadja again, had to standby on that fearful night and witness her mother's anguish when those same guns were turned on the boys.

Nadja's little brothers were shepherds heading sheep one day, and playing in their beloved mountains. Then suddenly, they were regarded as grown men and enemies of the Islamic State. A state that they knew nothing about.

Yousif and Walid had been little fighters until the end. When Yousif had taken that first step, and had broken away from Rooba's arms, everything seemed to move in slow motion.

He confronted their attackers with such courage, but, he was shot immediately and Nadja could still hear and see the pieces of his brain smeared on the neighbor's car.

Her younger brother Walid, now in the hands of ISIS captors would suffer terribly for the rest of his life, even if he wasn't shot down in the front lines. He would even have to kill Yezidis. He was too young to understand his fate. There would never be a sufficient explanation for any of it.

He would have to kill innocent people or be killed. He would be so destroyed that he would never be the same. They would have to walk by each other as loving strangers to make it through this ordeal.

But Nadja could sense her mother's love like a warm blanket with one glance. Neither of them had any contact with Nasima and she had been shipped away with a total stranger to God knows where, for only God knows what.

She would not allow herself think about her mother's forced rape and actions with this monster, but instead chose to just remembered her mother's loving acts of kindness to her father and the children.

GOING EAST

Nadja's ears had become accustomed to hearing the lock click loudly on the door every night when the men had had their fill of the girls held captive. That heinous sound had rang through the compound each and every night reminding her of the filthy prison in which she and the other were held.

She waited night after night to hear the door shut after the last soldier left and not hear the sound of the lock. Each night they came into her area. Sometimes two or three at a time.

Many times just one after another until she lost count. On one horrible occasion she had lost count after 21 men had viciously had their way with her. Everything imaginable was done to her sexually. Sometimes there were two men at a time. They wanted rape her of her soul.

She lay prostate for several days. Thankfully no one came to her as she lay in a pile of dirty rags. There was no comfort. Death was mocking her and the other girls.

But soon the line up began again. She would long for the last one to finish so that she could wait for the sound. He had decided that night to wake her up at roughly 2:00 AM, and continued to abuse and beat her until 3:30 or so.

He made guttural sounds so the profanities weren't as poignant, but his fists made their point. She understood the every punch and the systematic cruelty well by now. Then, laughingly, her last abuser pulled up his pants, lit a cigarette, and said then something to her in Arabic as he left.

Nadja was not sure from where this intense well of courage was springing up. However, she could not any longer ignore the fact that she wanted to get away from the animals that were stealing her body and her soul.

If she we're going to die, she would gladly die leaving the place of her captivity with some level of dignity and honor. She was bent on honoring her own life and taking from them the satisfaction of them using her for a human sperm bank even one more night.

She tiptoed to a small forced worship area where there was some water on hand. She tried frantically to scrub some of the filthy residue off of her legs and buttocks that was left behind by her captors.

Morning would break soon and she wanted to keep moving as quickly as possible. She desperately needed to bathe and then quietly tear a rag from a dirty sheet to help contain the bleeding from her vagina and rectum, with no one suspecting.

Her next move was to try the door. It was unlocked and just waiting to be opened. A blaze of victory and excitement ran through her so fiercely, that she would remember that feeling for the rest of her life.

Her adrenalin levels were spiked, but she had to think smart and not allow herself to run in a confused frenzy from the people and prison that attempted to make her nothing but property.

She then slipped through the doorway and dropped down on all fours to crawl out. She could hear them talking in a soldiers' space behind the compound. She could only hope that every one of them were congregated back there, but at this point she didn't care.

Nadja, by some powerful, unknown force knew that this would be hr one and only chance to gain her freedom. She had simply to crawl to a hidden spot behind another building. Although in great pain, she moved stealthily like a cat, and then cautiously rose up and began to walk.

Every step was painful with her whole body, hurting but she was responding to the sweet invitation of freedom. She was afraid for her life and flooded with great expectation at the same time. The combination felt delicious as her dream had finally come true. This whole area had been occupied by ISIS.

They were ruthless and had destroyed most of the ancient artifacts of this city. It was not known to Nadja at the time that Kurdish fighters had invaded and had taken back Raqqa from the extremists. She had no way of knowing, as the Yezidi women and girls had been cut off from all outside news.

Yet, the threats were still very real in the area. The land mines were planted everywhere and would later take a company and many workers to unearth them.

They were being held in a stronghold by animals who didn't even have power over the area anymore. She would find out later that the area had been taken back some months ago.

This had been the declared their caliphate "capital" and they had been ruthless in their undertaking even destroying a mosque. It had not been strict enough for them in their perception of what a religious extreme dogma should represent. They had changed even their own rules

She was finally taking flight, Nadja kept looking over her shoulder. She hid behind rocks and made sure that no one had followed her. She did not even want any of the girls to follow her as they would slow her down on this sacred mission. She had also, in her haste to leave the chamber of horrors, forgotten her shoes.

She was barely able to walk barefoot, and her feet were getting sliced like raw meat. She found comfort at the waters of the Euphrates and there is where she had to cross.

There had been no food or water brought along as she had to simply vanish from her attackers. There was no time to seek out provisions. She would have been caught and beaten to the very inch f her life.

Although weak, she was determined to keep heading east and then south, where the safety to at least breathe again would lie.

CHAPTER EIGHT

"AMIR"

" You have been assigned this mountain to show others it can be moved"

Unknown

Kurdistan was formed out of sheer necessity. Yet, The Kurds have always been known to demonstrate a heartfelt compassion for all people who are not threats. They even take no joy in defending Kurdistan to their death or their enemy's. The embrace of all people comes from possibly being starved, attacked and threatened with extinction.

They have suffered tremendously throughout their past with massive casualties from many outlying villages. Scores of people from all over the middle east chased the Kurds and they picked up their families and fled to one country or another.

They were handed death sentences by one group or another and there was only one option to survive. They had to scatter to various other parts of the region, and never really welcomed by their equally nefarious neighbors.

For centuries The Kurds have been under attack. People from various countries and factions had it in for the people who stood strong and maintained their culture. The Kurdish people knew what it was like to have their lives and destinies disrupted.

Any Kurdish man who prided himself on being a husband and a father knew deep inside that he could not protect his own family from Saddam Hussein's regime. Every Kurdish man had felt less like a man every day of his existence in Northern IRAQ.

Every Kurdish man knew what it was like to be hunted and if they were not running with their families, their villages were being destroyed for no apparent reason; every house. The violations that occurred were gut wrenching, with no one there to stop the regime.

They survived many attacks and had to form a strong autonomous army, but each aggression against them was keenly worse than the ones before. They had to rely on their own strength as outside armies would always arrive too late. The onslaught was always quick and aggressive. The casualties were too numerous to document.

Saddam Hussein was one of the worst nemeses, that the Kurds had to encountered historically. He was a brutal dictator that killed even his own people, and a butcher who would still live fresh in the minds and stories of the Kurdish People for decades to come.

Schools had dedicated songs to him and if anyone spoke ill Of Saddam and hid regime, they would be reported and killed instantly. This went for everyone, but he especially had it in for the Kurds.

He was known to go from village to village and kill Kurds just for the sake of killing them. He would kidnap young Kurdish girls walking home from school or the market, rape and murder them and they were never seen again by their families.

However, when this happened the Peshmerga would make their way from a cave at night and kill many of Saddam's soldiers with surprise attacks.

The Kurds fought back from the mountains. Saddam's Army was fierce. The Peshmerga would make them pay dearly their own retribution with blood shed from unsuspecting IRAQI soldiers. this did nothing but anger Saddam even more.

This didn't sit well with the evil dictator. No one was allowed to challenge his murderous and oppressive ways. and he would make them pay anyway that he could.

He was an ego maniac with a beastly and devious approach to anyone who would dare go up against him. They were punished in ways that the world still knows noting about.

The Kurds had the good fortune of having the United States of America and other European Nations intervene. Being backed up against the mountains with no food or water brought sure starvation to Kurdish men, women and children. Saddam was plotting to exterminate the Kurds with his weapons of mass destruction.

They were real, whether the world believed it or not. Syria is where they ended up and the people there who suffered from the deadly gas attacks can attest that Saddam had an arsenal of deadly weapons to kill the Kurds at will if launched.

Fortunately for the Kurds America's intervention by George W. Bush and the American Congress was right on time. Food was flown in along with water and other supplies. So much was dropped that people were even killed by the large quants that were distributed.

Yet, with almost 200,000 Kurds still missing, with absolutely no word of what had really happened to them, or if they are currently living or indeed dead, the peace that they seek fosters a hope coupled with despair.

Saddam had come to the end of his beastly rope and had decided to kill all of the remaining Kurds with deadly gases and other weapons. But, to his military disadvantage, the American Armed forces showed up and Saddam was finally captured, tried and hanged.

Yet after The Kurdish Army, better known as the Peshmerga, had taken on Saddam and the IRAQI Forces, with the help of America, a new found freedom erupted.

The Kurds rejoice the region was now free from the "Butcher of Baghdad. He died infamous for his butchering and rapes that he and his sons had inflicted upon the whole Region of Kurdistan.

The Peshmerga soldiers had been fighting aggressively to maintain this fragile freedom and had finally seen a new day, when a new threat had been introduced to the region.

Although it had been over 20 years since his overthrow, death, destruction, and the disappearance of many Kurds per family, were constantly in the backs of the minds of the people. Also, the many languages that they were forced to learn, reminded of the fight for their very lives in this region.

Iran had prohibited Kurdish to be spoken even if it was their mother tongue, so many Kurdish children grew up only speaking Arabic, Persian or what is known as Farsi. Along with many other dialects of languages, which strips a people of any cohesion, Arabic was forced within IRAQ by Saddam Hussein.

They were few in numbers and weakened by previous defense measures, but they were still wholly committed to protecting everyone in the Region of Kurdistan, at all costs, from any demonic invaders.

They protected Christians, different sects of Muslims, Assyrians, and any Jews that were left in the region. The Kurds had experienced every moment of this horror with Saddam Hussein.

Only there was a new group formed from the old groups which had new weapons and a terroristic ideology which the world had not yet encountered. They are the group which is referred to as "ISIS".

The Kurds had always enjoyed some form of backup no matter if there where religious or racial differences, but this time they were on their own. They depended on their army called the Peshmerga and weapons that were given to them by George W. Bush in 1991. It seemed that they were no match for the invading enemy.

However, contrary to popular belief, each man and boy knew the mountains and the caves like the back of their hands. They reigned down terror on the terrorists and took back villages and cities. Each battle costs lives and futures, but the Peshmerga fought on.

Each one of the Peshmerga's soldiers who had known what it was like to be threatened with death, or had already lost many family members, and were so willing to help other groups who were being attacked.

What happened to others had a serious affect on the outcome on an entire region. The beginning of the Peshmerga Forces date all the way back to the early 1940s. The handwriting was on the wall that there would be trouble for the Kurdish People, and there was plenty.

This Kurdish Military was forced to mobilize as a movement to form a resistance to the centralized Iraqi state. Since then it has become essential to flow with a momentum of growth in size, strength in the structure, and sophistication in its fighting capabilities.

The Saddam Hussein era was shocked by a dramatic growth in the size of the force of the Peshmerga, and they eventually led Kurdistan to quasi-autonomy. They had a new found nationalism inspired by the unity that was acquired to survive.

The Iraqi constitution has incorporated extremely precise terminology in its own provisions for integrating secondary forces into its own army. They want other forces to join them but refuse to consider the Peshmerga an integral an primary fighting force of IRAQI Kurdistan.

They would never be denied. This means that the terminology that has defined the Peshmerga has been essential for marking out their future position in the Iraqi security force.

However, the argument over the clarity of the terminology in regards to the Peshmerga is the starting point to debating the legitimacy and conditions of their integration.

In other words, IRAQ can set its own determinants for its armed forces but if there is another joining force there are strict conditions to whether or not they can join or even exist, and as a viable army, hate being referred to as a "secondary militia".

The Peshmerga, for the most part, has had to just ignore their unclear politics and conditions. They would not bow to any enemies or to the Centralized Government.

There was never any real trust established, as they had been lied to over and over, costing many lives. The Kurds found it in their best interest to depend on themselves and on keep their fighting forces strong and independent.

There are two main parties in the Kurdish Government, but despite their differences within Kurdistan, all the political parties have seemed to find common grounds in facing Baghdad, when they perceive the specificity of Peshmerga questioned or the interests of Iraqi Kurdistan under threat.

The Kurdistan Regional Government has always been the most compromising of the the two governments entities and were always willing to integrate their forces or work along side Baghdad.

Yet, they could not conceive of accepting conditions that would weaken their defense forces where Kurdistan was involved.

A formal and gradual agreement could only be conceived in the long term provided that the Peshmerga will always get to keep their current military hierarchy, their training centers, and their specific location in the Kurdistan region.

This principled agreement has won the Peshmerga the right to work with the Iraqi security forces without dismantling either one of them. This made it possible for the Peshmerga to be independent but still depend on their salaries from Baghdad.

The Kurdish government has benefited some but very little from the Iraqi Ministry of Defense's budget and the Peshmerga have had to train and equip their own soldiers. This has left them with the disadvantage of holding on and fixing their fighting relics to be armed at all.

Many feel that this was probably the plan of the IRAQIs so as not make the fighting machine, the Peshmerga stronger and more viable. The plan has not succeeded, however, as the Peshmerga took on the well armed ISIS soldiers and won battle after battle.

They have not desired necessarily to train in the Iraqi military academies, as thePeshmerga train their own fighters and have already proven to be some of the world's top fighters.

Finally, The Kurdish Regional Government has been cautious about joining formally with IRAQ and the force remained substantively at the disposal of the KRG, in case tensions between Baghdad and Erbil were to rise again.

Even Baghdad has had to admit that the Kurdish Peshmerga are excellent in maintaining Kurdistan's safety for its citizens and they grant the Peshmerga their deepest respect.

Although it is still not formally considered a "nation" as sorts, it is a viable region that has taken on the likes of ISIS with demonstrated success after success in the bloody battles.

The Kurds have joined and took action to have an autonomous area in which to survive with the dream of one day formulating a real and viable nation built solely on peace, but Arabs in the region are fighting this notion with all of their might.

Turkey survives on refining the oil from the Kurdish oil wells and with full autonomy this would cease. This would mean the loss of millions of dollars for Turkey in annual revenues. Iran sells goods to the Kurds from Tehran, and IRAQ is aggressive with high taxes excised on the Kurdish People and their businesses.

Things are constantly in the process of changing but so slowly that Kurdistan is still surrounded by enemies who would seek their demise. The Kurds fight for their existence in between countries who rulers would seize the inexhaustible trade routes, and the precious resources like oil and spring water which is abundant throughout the area.

The Islamic State and the Levant or ISIS has changed the scope of the Middle East entirely. It was born and began serious recruiting in 1999.

ISIS is determined to bring a radical Islam to the whole region, but Kurdistan has fought and won many hard battles to not allow the abject force of a radical sect of religion to be shoved down the throats of the Kurds and anyone else who resides in Kurdistan.

IRAQ , as a whole, was in grave danger and Baghdad insisted that The Peshmerga deploy forces not only within the Kurdistan Region, but also beyond the borders, in the disputed territories of Ninevah, Diyala, Kirkuk and Salahuddin provinces. They battled and won with weapons dating back to 1991.

Now, along with their lengthy history, their victories and martyrs, there is a real and genuinely structured organization. Their noted and well earned official role in Iraqi security, has made many Kurds feel proud but extremely angered when anyone refers to the Peshmerga as anything other than a genuine fighting force.

However, with all of the victories against ISIS in the region, the Peshmerga were desperately called upon by the Yezedis to help them in their fight against ISIS.

The Peshmerga, strained by horrible economic and old weapons from 1991, were indeed the only hope by which all of Kurdistan, including the Yezidis, could be protected.

But Sinjar was attacked, plundered, many men murdered and women and children kidnapped, as the Peshmerga were busy in many other cities and villages trying to contain ISIS who actually had American modern weapons.

They had a small band of fighters, but they would be all killed by the scores of ISIS militants who invaded their village with state of the art weaponry.

When the terrible invasion took place the Yezidis found themselves all alone and at the mercy of blood thirsty radicals. There was no mercy, only random killings and rapes.

The Peshmerga would have been more than happy to go in and fight that band of terrorists, but were ill equipped to engage in such a momentous undertaking and would have lost many, too many soldiers of their own to keep Kurdistan.

The order came from Erbil and the Kurdish soldiers were directed to stand down and move away from Sinjar at the time of the ISIS invasion in August 2014. This brave group of soldiers were short of ammunition, manpower, and strength.

The Kurdish Government forbid them to enter into a full-scale war over the Yezidis and their village. The order had been given by the hands of the Kurdish government and the Peshmerga were instructed to stand down.

This order came to the dismay of many of the Peshmerga on that morning, because they had developed a heart felt commiseration with every tribe and group in Kurdistan. These fighting soldiers did not want to see any group within the bounds of Kurdistan destroyed.

The people of Kurdistan were helpless to assist and heartbroken to think that the Yezidi People were so being so brutally attacked. The ones who would survive the massacre were led away to compounds in Syria, or starved in the mountains if they had made it to safety.

What was worse than slow starvation was the idea of being taken by this band of degenerates. ISIS whole deprived method of torture was to abduct, abuse and kill their victims while filming these grotesque acts for the world to see.

Many all over the world had already shockingly witnessed ISIS radicals beheading people who were not of like minds and similar beliefs. In fact, there were no similar beliefs as the savage anti kept going up with money and power being their sole objective.

These images were striking fear in hearts and lives of everyone who watched the world over. This meant that all people in the region who did not join with them in their movement of blood and terror were in harm's way.

The horrible fact remained that these images were unbelievable but real, and staged to invoke fear. They were filmed and dispersed though the likes of YouTube, and the world stood by watching and waiting to see who would come to the aid of whole group of people that ISIS had killed or captured.

In reality the world was waiting to see if these religious extremists would soon be at their doorstep, and if they were allowed to proceed who would stop them?

For the brave men and women of the Peshmerga who risked their lives and even sacrificed salaries to buy their own bullets, their homes and the lives of their children, there is no way to put into words their courage and zeal to defend the Region. At that time, the Peshmerga was all the world had.

They fought and continue to fight with every drop of courage and strength their hearts can summon. Each man felt it his responsibility to face the real pressures of maintaining the safety of the Region. Each man's family and Kurdistan are of the utmost importance. This was especially transparent in the life of a formidable young soldier named, Amir.

THE MEETING

Amir had joined the Peshmerga when he was 18 years old. He was not only courageous but extremely intelligent for his young years. He chose to enlist in the The Kurdish Army, called The Peshmerga. He had finished his secondary education but chose to bypass his free college education.

He was at the top of his class and he could have chosen any college in Kurdistan to equip himself for his future, but instead he was insisting that he be stationed near Mosul where the toughest fighting was taking place.

He was strikingly handsome with jet black air and penetrating green eyes. He had a thick mustache even though he was only in his early twenties. Amir was a beautiful specimen if a man.

Amir was tall and carried himself in a distinguished manner. He was good looking, and respected by all of the other soldiers that he fought alongside, even though he was just a young man.

His rugged body was developed from climbing the mountain since he had been a young boy. Going up steep slopes was sport for the Kurdish youths. Each Friday was also spent picnicking in the mountains. Children played on the slopes while the women laid out the weekend feast.

Each day a group would get together and find a high peak to conquer. Up there they would smell the flowers, the spices that grew wild, and pick mushrooms for them mothers and grandmothers.

Each day was filled with physical activity in Kurdistan as young people did not sit around and watch TV. That was because electricity was scarce and in the springtime and the fall the weather invites each man woman and child to experience the beautiful nature.

His soft eyes and good looks were not to be confused with his warrior instincts, as he had much experience in fighting under his belt. ISIS was never to be underestimated and yet, Amir had handled his part in the present war quite heroically.

Amir was extremely intelligent, on and off the field. He could have chosen to become anything and anyone that he had wanted to be. His discipline and humility stood as shining symbols. He could learn as well as teach. He ate training manuals for his mental sustenance.

He had learned from his Commanders as a son learns from his father. It was not about war they were fighting, but about peace and security. They were in indeed fighting proudly for the future of Kurdistan.

He was definitely the epitome of a young man of excellent character. His quality in decisive decision making on the battlefield in his daily life made him a young man of great significance in Kurdistan. Young men his age looked up to him and his relatives in the cities and in the villages loved to speak his name.

He had chosen to serve his people with a love that was not only skilled but intelligent. Amir was closely acquainted with the the atrocities that the Kurdish people had met along their journey to have their own nation and freedom. He was a boy who had tuned into a man characterized with bigger dreams than he himself would ever dare to dream.

Amir woke up every morning excited about serving his people. Everything in his life was centered around conserving the land for future generations. Although, Kurdistan was surrounded by mountains, groups also wanted to surround them, and were determined to stop any progress that the Kurdish people would make.

It was an excruciating reality to know that the neighbors who surrounded Kurdistan; Turkey, Iran, Syria and even Southern IRAQ, were not comfortable with Kurdistan being a sovereign place where courage would ultimately determine destiny. The surrounding nations would never not want to relinquish their hold.

They were perfectly content in seeing ISIS invade Kurdistan and drain the economy and all of its resources to continue their quest for survival. Still soldiers like Amir fought on brilliantly with the Peshmerga realizing victory after impossible victory.

He was adamant about avenging his beloved Kurdistan. He wanted to see a Region and he and his family had personally suffered with the loss of his only sister. He lived and breathed to avenge any other hurting woman that he would ever come into contact with.

War was a dirty business, and he knew this. But he also swore that his family's tears would not be in vain. Their loss spurred him on to defend Kurdistan and right whatever injustices that he could in the process. There was plenty of opportunity for the latter.

Enemies surrounded the four Regions that made up Kurdistan, and each ought to keep Kurdistan dependent on surrounding countries for food, clothes and just plain necessities.

Yet, even more, Amir had the sad personal knowledge of losing a loved one to the several IRAQI Army soldiers who had kidnapped his sister many years before. She was still spoken of as one speaks about an angel

Amir was an overcomer and wanted to pursue freedom not just for his family, but for all of the Kurdish people. He vowed in his heart to let no obstacle stand in his way. He had been brutally beaten by his father almost daily, who drank plenty, cheated on his mother and seemed to hate himself. It was not entirely his fault, however. He had just given up hoping for a future in Kurdistan.

And after all of their painful existing his mother was the surviving parent and she was in pieces. Their father had just dropped dead one day from lung cancer. He was severely agitated and smoked up to 4 packs of cigarettes a day. Amir never found out the reasons for his father's anger.

The man could never open up about his deep wounds, but Amir speculated it was from his family having to flee from place to place for refuge when the Kurds were being assailed and fleeing for their lives.

Amir's mother and the older people of their family lived with a painful memory and he could not remember a day that went by that the mother didn't have to be consoled from crying. That had happened some 24 years prior, but for their family it was just like yesterday.

The father reacted quite a bit differently. He constantly took his pain out on his wife and children. Amir was beaten hard and frequent. Perhaps it was because of oppression of others who were friends and relatives, or because of his own deep grief.

Perhaps Amir's father felt totally responsible for what had happened to their sister. He never spoke of the incident, but there it was burning in his heart. He had no way to cope with his grief and blamed himself for her being missing.

The family prohibited anyone to speak of her as if she were dead. She was spoken of in a present tense which would somehow kept their frail hopes alive.

If Amir's mother had assured the father that there would not have been any way to go up against those soldiers, he would weep, but later that night a beating would follow. She lost hope daily of her daughter and husband returning to her.

It is one thing to know of the neighbor's misfortune, but quite another to lose a child, and in your dreams you hear her screaming for help. Dilara's kidnapping was beyond belief for Amir's family.

Amir's sister, Dilara, a precious daughter was a beautiful young teenager, with a bright future ahead of her. As bright as anyone's future could be when armies are at you back.

She was a top student, fluent in Kurdish and Arabic. She worked hard to keep her scores in math and science and was genuinely loved by her classmates. They too were shattered when they heard the news.

Dilara loved going to the market and making purchases for her mother for the family dinner. This give her an opportunity to see her friends and laugh with them for a while. They would catch up on all of the news of their school classmates. Sometimes she would even take this news home when she would find out someone elderly in their Village had died.

She just happened to be walking on a village road by herself to go in which their mother had cautioned her not to take because of the dangers of Saddam's soldiers. She was happy and carefree taking a shortcut to see her friend at a nearby village when the truck drove by.

She hadn't even noticed their jeers and laughter. They turned the truck around, and the soldiers asked her where she was going in Arabic. They could see that she was a beautiful Kurdish girl, and the rest was painful history.

She was taken and never heard from again. She had been a Kurdish victim of the soldiers of Saddam. They thought of the beautiful Kurdish gils as a special prize and would kidnap them at will.

The Peshmerga forces when they would find out would then launch attacks on random IRAQI soldiers, who would pay the price for their insidious comrades' crimes

Amir could not run home to be comforted by his mother as she too was suffering with no one else to turn to. There were other children to care for. She just kept repeating that she hoped peace would come to all of the Kurdish People.

After all, she would naturally want a good future for her children, and she was very proud of Amir being aggressive about his involvement in securing a future for the Region. Yet, she feared for his life each and every day.

This troubled Amir and he had been proud to serve in the Peshmerga, but equally happy to escape his home life which was dismal. It was a home that had tears dripping from every curtain. There was no way to fix all that happened.

Each day was more volatile and depressing than the one before. There was not a lot to do or look forward to. Amir was seeking some rewards for the pressures and pains of just being Kurdish.

The wars and constant battles were a brutal game of cat and mouse. It became necessary to survey the enemy, take an inventory of their weapons and learn where they would bury mines to destroy trucks from moving in on them. Amir was brilliant at protecting his fellow soldiers and determining where the danger lie.

He had developed instincts from trying to avoid the daily beatings from his father who was vexed. He moved like a cat. He was cautious but courageous, seemingly fearing nothing.

He used brute force on the enemy and when needed, he his own soldiers conditioned to back up when information was going to be extracted during a capture. He showed the no mercy when getting what he needed from ISIS soldiers by way of intelligence.

He trusted no one that had their sights set on destroying Kurdistan, but he also had a sense of compassion for the young boys who ISIS had forced into their service. They came from many walks of life and if ISIS had captured them they were subject to the most inhuman tortures including homosexual acts.

Amir could feel compassion, but he couldn't allow anyone or anything to take him off guard. The slightest mistake and ISIS would move in for the kill, and if they were captured, their heads would literally be sent home to their families in a bag.

Their missions called for no mistakes along the way. Taking caution under any and all circumstances was a highly cherished attribute. These Lions were not only patient but shrewd. They moved in a distinct way as to remind their enemies that the Peshmerga were as cunning as they ever thought that they could be. God was on their side and it was evident.

Nadja was just one of many young women who had been taken to Raqqa, Syria. She had never been sold, but raped so many times that she could not possibly keep an account of how many men had entered her body. She had killed each man in her mind as many times as she had been used and discarded. She had escaped when so many were still be held captive.

Many others had already taken their own lives unable to cope with the grotesque circumstances that grew worse by the day. Still others had returned to their villages only to be rejected by those who felt that the conditions of ISIS had so stained the lives of the young girls that they wanted nothing to do with them.

If they returned with a child, they and the child would be ostracized. The baby would be from the loins of ISIS or some stranger in which the young girl was sold.

Nadja had made a run for it and nothing or no one would get in her way. She was breathing fresh freedom and her revenge was in the face that she would not be touched by these cruel animals ever again. She had taken off running tasting victory in every step.

After a brief moment of fear filling her legs, strength came from a source that she could not identify. She was heading toward some surviving cousins or friends in a small village where other Yezidis had made it to safety.

She didn't know how she would get there, only that she had to keep on moving ahead one step at a time. Food and water were a distant thought in her mind. The fresh air and no one claiming her body for that moment was incentive enough.

It was then she happened to run up upon on some of the Peshmerga Soldiers that had been patrolling in the area. They were alerted that someone was coming their way and that person could be strapped with bombs. ISIS sympathizers had no love for the Peshmerga and were ready to die for what they felt was their religious duty.

The Peshmerga took no time in mobilizing for an attack from this woman running at them. They would shoot to kill rather than risk the lives of the Peshmerga who were losing troops on the roads from the surprise car bombings and ambushes.

Nadja had not responded to any of their commands as she was incoherent with thirst and hunger at this point. When they had told her in Kurdish to wait, she just kept on advancing.

They were hoping that she somehow understood how urgent the situation was. Instead, she picked up a dead branch and began to wave it in the air.

She held the tiny branch, wielding it like a knife for over two hours, while Amir and the other soldiers had tried to calm her. She was filthy and crying.

She was through with the beatings and with being a human ashtray. She refused to be hurt again, even if it meant death. Nadja had nothing to lose at this point.

Miraculously, Amir called out to the troops to wait. They did not want this event to result in the killing of a young woman, but if it would secure the area, they would blow her to bits. She had been far enough away that if she detonated any device it would not affect the camp of the soldiers.

On the command and plea of Amir, contrary to their instincts, they waited. The were told to stand down until further orders were issued. He wanted a better look at this wandering person. It was a young girl, but she either had to be very courageous or crazy. This was ISIS territory.

There was no explanation for their hesitation outside of their hands being held by a power higher than theirs. They still shouted commands at her in the Kurdish that she was somewhat familiar with, and she was able to make out most of the high toned statements in Kurdish.

The compassion in Amir's voice cut right through the confusion. He could see that she was in distress and meant no harm. She was dusty from the long walk and the tear stains altered their ideas of a suicide bomber as there was no anger or hostility.

She could immediately sense the irony as she felt his fingers take the branch tenderly from her hand. Hungry, exhausted and alone she was determined, if it cost her very life, to get away from the savages that had stolen her past. When she could tilt her head up, she saw eyes that told a tale of compassion.

Amir was kind and gentle and earnestly wanted to know who this young stranger could be and where did she come from. She had braved an escape and he and the other soldiers could not miss the sights and sounds of someone who looked like they had just escaped from being housed in a cage. And unfortunately it was an ISIS cage.

Nadja hadn't really noticed how handsome and kind this soldier was. She had been walking for hours. She had briefly attempted to look over her shoulder to see if any of the ISIS soldiers had followed her, but she just ran knowing that freedom was now hers and time was of the essence.

She was delirious and she believed that she had to just kept on running. She stumbled and she fell many times trying to get as far away from the compound as she could. The fresh air touched her skin and she felt alive for the first time in a year. She was running for her life and she knew it.

Amir was the one who was willing to get a closer look at this young woman who had endured such an heart wrenching experience. He could see the blood running to her ankles. She was young woman who had been ravished and he could only think of his sister that he never got to know.

He broke down in front of the other soldiers with such bitter weeping that the whole group stepped back and dropped their heads. His crying was like a bitter song that flowed to his mother and sister admitting that he could finally relate to their deepest sorrows.

They were inviting her to walk through a door that she could barely believe to be real, although it had only been one year ago. A door of of safety and comfort. He was a Kurd in the Peshmerga. He was a Muslim, and she had no other recourse but to trust him and the other soldiers. She was in another difficult situation.

Nadja had to depend now on this Muslim man and his forces if she wanted to live. She had no other choice. However, Nadja was so starved for some kind of compassion that she slowly began to respond to Amir's kindness.

She sensed a well of mercy springing up from within him. After being abandoned and abused, Nadja sensed real love flowing from a man that she had never met before, nor would in previous circumstances ever have the opportunity to make his sweet acquaintance.

She also had a slight etherial sense of destiny as to their meeting. As she fled on foot from Raqqa, Syria, she could have encountered any number of people. Some of these people could have attacked her, or even returned her to ISIS, but she ran into this group of Peshmerga instead and even though she was very young, she translated this event into something heaven sent.

Nadja decided right then and there that every one of Amir's hot tears would not fall to the ground in vain. She would fight to live and maybe someday even love again with a love that passes human understanding.

In such a short time that she had encountered this precious man, Amir had been her greatest teacher. He was living proof that people can manifest a human compassion and integrity that goes beyond cultures and religion. He could not have been kinder to Nadja.

Amir and Nadja's world collided. They were experiencing strange feelings at an even stranger time. They were thrown together by sheer fate. Nadja cold not believe that she would ever trust any man again, but Amir was different.

His presence was overwhelming. He was masculine with the most tender heart she ever experienced. He was her knight with the most shining armor. She believed him. His eyes and smile were sincere. He seemed unaffected by all of his trials. He was her melody.

The soldiers, however, were not pleased with Nadja being in their area and the private time that the two spent on the last night before she would be delivered to Sege.

But, she was invited to sit and eat with Amir. He shared his food with her like she was a young child. She enjoyed every bite, and at the same time savoring the moments.

She was safe, warm, and trying to remember the last time that she got to eat anything in peace. Tonight she would eat under the stars and there would be no one to hurt her.

The soldiers were not pleased with the private time that the two spent taking on their last night together, but did not dare confront Amir. They held the deepest respect for him and trusted his judgement.

This was not customary, for a woman and man to spend private time together that was not married, but nothing that was happening at that moment was conventional.

They took a long walk and had an intense conversation that was so badly needed by both of them. There was a sweet relief as they shared their pain and small joys.

Each was interested in the other's stories. They talked about their sweet childhood memories and what and who had invaded their lives. Peace was always a far off concept and never obtained, as war was always prevalent in their realty.

They shared how they both had lost loved ones. Some were killed recently, others were slaughtered over time. Somehow, the sadder the conversation grew, their hearts were filled with hope. They were evaluating their short lives and concluded that they were left on earth for some higher purpose.

But something else was taking place. As they spoke about their past and every obstacle that had confronted both cultures, something was transpiring between them and they both knew it. Amir had witnessed something that caused him great joy.

There was no way to describe what was filling his heart. He had made Nadja smile. It was an uncertain smile but not forced. She was indeed at peace and their little meeting had brought her pleasure.

They would not give up on their quest for a brighter future although neither one of them knew what lie ahead. Every day had been brutal up to that point, but just for a few rare moments they were content.

THE RITE OF PASSAGE

Amir was going to see her to safety at any cost. He figured that she had been through enough, and she didn't even have a family member that she could contact. She was visually all alone.

Amir now had to contact Command as he would never disobey orders. He had to try and explain to his Commander a strange story about he and his group of soldiers found a victim of ISIS wandering in their area.

Although, ISIS soldiers had been killed or captured, but the area was in the process of being secured. There was no way to assess all of the circumstances that were surrounding the Peshmerga Forces. They were working on trying to establish some security in the area especially on the major routes.

The Commanders were busy trying bring order and restoration to the ravaged areas especially near Mosul. Refugees were everywhere fleeing to surrounding cities and villages. People had lost their homes, hearts and even their lives to a group of destroyers who could never even agree on their purpose.

They looted every group that was in their way. They had no objective but to strike fear into the hearts of the people with a flimsy religious excuse, and with their stakes and people losing their houses and homes they were on a frantic search to find safety. The Peshmerga made it possible for people to find new dealings.

One city in Kurdistan, called Duhok, absorbed a total of number refugees that was compared to its own population. People slept in mosques, churches, rooftops and any other place they could find safety.

The Regional Kurdish Government made it mandatory for its citizens to help with any and all resources. All racial, cultural and religious walls disintegrated as people helped one another. But it was huge undertaking and camps had to established at the drop of a hat.

Nadja was just one of many people who had lost family, friends and her home. To ask the Commanders that they may escort this one individual to a predetermined destination was gong to be a presumptuous question.

Amir was so highly respected that his Commanders were willing to listen. He had never been arbitrary. Also, he would never jeopardize the lives of his fellow officers. He was the epitome of an excellent soldier, who could follow as well as lead.

His Commander, after giving this request careful consideration and voicing his objections, gave Amir an opportunity to give reasonable answers. Amir answered his concerns and the Commander gave him permission to escort Nadja to a village called Sege. The Commander even concluded that this brave woman was also "Kurdistan". She ws a brave fighter.

It was predominantly a Christian village, but the Yezidi community found solace there. They had fled their villages but they found welcoming arms, food and half made shelters. There were no doors or windows on the unfinished houses, but they were sustainable.

Nadja was brought into Sege by the Peshmerga and was welcomed and celebrated in a strange manner. She had survived ISIS and defeated their plans and probably her demise. She was alive and if she would allow these circumstances to work in her favor, she could begin again.

CHAPTER NINE

"ELZA"

"We must become the change was seek in the world."
Gandhi

THE JOURNEY

Nadja was naturally suspicious and curious at the same time. She felt a little more secure in the clinic each day. It was going to take some time and that was all that she had now.

She had plenty of time to think and hopefully a time to do some healing. But in the meantime, she would not allow her guard to be let down or one moment. She as going to be born again to be able to trust as she could not afford one more disappointment. If she was tormented in more more area of her life, she didn't how she would survive it.

She took care to watch Elza for one wrong move. Her mistrust was a defense weapon she relied on to see if she could "catch" someone like Elza in the very act of being deceptive.

She could not figure out what made Elza "tick". She was utterly and completely abandoned to her work. A work that carried with it such a deep responsibility for human souls.

Her work was one that held such little hope. Even the most dedicated and optimistic person would find devoting time to care for these victims extremely difficult.

Yet, her work was not clinic analysis but institute and Nadja doubted that Elza had learned how to "read" these patients from some class or manual. She felt every pain and hurt. She somehow grabbed their shame and moved it from them as far as he setting sun.

Yet, Elza was there, sincere and most of all really present. She possessed an uncanny ability to hear what was unspoken, and delve into hearts and lives to shake the foundations of every pain that gripped every tortured heart.

Nadja was curious to find out the source of this strength as Elza cared for her. Nothing passed her ability to "see" what the people who needed her selflessness was facing, absolutely nothing…day or night.

Elza was the most patient and kind lady Nadja had encountered since her mother. She really cared. She was a pillar of strength and encouragement, but at this point, Nadja trusted no one.

She finally came to the understanding that she sent here for reasons that were beyond what she could presently see. She confessed to herself that she could not make these steps all alone.

She was so desperately lonely for her family who were killed or who had disappeared. Nadja was so afraid of living, but with all that she had been through, she knew that she was not meant to die.

It was a warm Saturday afternoon soon after that Nadja decided to go out try the garden atmosphere. She could be alone and smell the essences of nature. They filled her senses. The putrid odors etched in her mind of the compound were fought of with the delicate aroma's of roses and the pines.

She she had just began to close her eyes when she heard footsteps coming toward her and she looked up in time to see that it was Elza. Nadja was relieved and and as always, Elza was beaming with a tender smile that never seemed to leave her face.

"Hello, Elza. Where are you off to?", asked Nadja softly. Elza had never wasted one minute that Nadja could remember. But deep in her heart she was hoping that Elza would just spend a few minutes with her in the garden.
"Why, I was just looking for you", Elza said in a soft voice.
"You were looking for me?", Nadja replied in a surprised tone.
"Why yes! I saw that you were not in your room, so I decided to go out and look for you. I know the places where you may be resting by now."

Nadja was extremely curious as to why Elza had sought her out, but on the other hand she was glad that someone who cared enough to look for her. Nadja was tired of being so private, and yet living as a public recluse, but there were so very few people in her life now that she could allow herself to trust.

"I think it's time that we talk Nadja," said Elza. "I see you the questions in your eyes every time I come to check on you, and I want to answer your questions so that you may know why I care for the people here the way that I do.

You are not alone in your questions and I honestly believe that if you have some answers you will embrace your healing. I need you to believe Nadja, that in many ways I am not different from you.

We come from different places, but really from the same set of circumstances. I want you to know that I will never compare my circumstances with yours, but when you hear my story will understand that I too had to seek comfort, or I would've lost my mind."

Nadja was listening intently. It was not often that people were willing to bear their souls, especially those who are part of administrative care.

She was not only curious but also aware that there would be a freedom that would far outweigh her dismal thinking. She had every right to feel the hopelessness and shame that her captors had instilled in her for a whole year.

She had come to a crossroads in her existence. Yet, hoping beyond hope, she longed for the day that she could slip out of her deep cavern of despair. She was so grateful that Elza wanted to share her story, even though it was filled with pain.

So, at least just for one day Nadja knew that if she could marginalize her own thoughts, float into Elza's world, and slip into an empathy mode she was going to learn a great deal.

Nadja wanted wanted Elza possessed. There was a freedom in the words that Elza had spoken. It was like they belonged to someone else. Like she was recanting the story of a complete stronger, but Nadja knew that its was hers. How could she disavow her own pain, she thought? It was going to take a well worked out formula, or maybe even a miracle.

ONE DARK NIGHT

Elza just happened to be a Christian and her faith was evident not only in the woods that she conveyed, but in her attitude towards not only the people who had come for healing, but the entire staff. Her love rose up over the people like a beautiful and protective cloud.

Nadja knew that she was unable to choose the time and space in which to fight the most important battle. She chose that particular day in time in which to open up her senses and cling to what might be. After all, she had nothing to lose. What she had to gain was not going to be temporal but everlasting.

Elza was about to unleash a new invisible pathway that led to a door. What was on the other side of that door only Nadja would be privy to. It was hers to open or forever stay shut. Nadja was forced to abandon her fears.

Freedom is a very clear idea. When compared to slavery freedom is always worth fighting for. Yet, it is birthed and centered around a variety of choices. Choices that would be extremely hard to make, but Nadja knew that if Elza could at least lead her to the path of understanding, she would be willing to take each small step.

With the sun high in the sky out in the garden Elza began to tell her story. Nadja knew instinctively that this would be a defining moment for her. She had been anticipating Elza's sharing her heart and this would be time well spent.

She wasn't sure that she was strong enough to walk into Elza's life adventure but somehow Nadja knew that the words would be rich and poignant. She was going to pay her closest attention.

This reenactment was going to be the one that would change her life forever, and she decided from the depths of her to hang on to every word. This would mean being pulled into someone else's deep cavern and not being able to get out. After all that she had experienced, she figured how bad could it get? She leaned in as Elza began to speak.

" It had happened to be an unseasonably warm night in June exactly four years ago when I had just left my mother's home, following a great dinner. My mother is one of the best cook's in southern Germany. That night she created all of our favorites. We all had eaten dinner until we were stuffed, and we laughed and laughed to relieve some of pressure of consuming too much food."

"We sat around and talked about the good old days when we were growing up. We got the cards out and played which was our family weekly tradition. It was a joyous time and yet not a holiday or any special occasion. Our family just loved to have get-togethers."

"My mother just sat and marveled at her grown children and how they saw the world so much differently than she did those many years ago."

When you watch her eyes you could see that she was thinking about how quickly the years have passed and how hard it was to raise five children after my father had passed away. After the last child he had only lived for two years and died from a massive heart attack because of working so hard.

Life was not easy in Germany after the war. People were trying to rebuild their lives and their country at the same time. He had not joined the Nazi Army because he was a skilled worker and his talents in manufacturing kept him out of the war.

This had been a blessing in disguise, as he would've never happen able to live with the memories of the atrocities that had haunted so many of his friends.

They had started out as young men together but got old before the years because of what the government had forced them to do. Many of their Jewish neighbors had disappeared, and so did the delis, pharmacies and magnificent violin music that came from the apartments where they all lived together.

"My brothers had come with their wives and had only one child between them. My two sisters were married with several children, but their husbands had stayed behind because of their heavy workload. That didn't matter as we all and all the little cousins were always ecstatic to see each other. My bothers' wives and I were the unofficial cleaning crew, and we always quietly disappeared into the kitchen."

While doing dishes and wrapping leftovers they told secrets about their home life. They were hilarious as they spoke about private matters concerning the men that I had grown up with.

"I have never been married so I just listened and thought thatI had plenty to learn. My brothers would continue sitting in the living room watching TV and talking about sports and hunting."

"We had all spent a marvelous day together. But, in reality, we knew it was that time which comes all too quickly when families are having a great time sharing memories."

"We needed to depart to our separate homes and go on with real life, and we surrounded our mother hugging her and reassuring her that each one would come back and check on her during the week. But that week would change all of our lives forever."

"I was so over stuffed with food that I opted to walk home to get some exercise and I wanted just to reflect on the day. We were all getting a little bit older, but I wanted to retreat to my childhood. My brothers, their wives and my sisters all begged me to get a lift home with them. "

"Not really wanting to offend any of them I chose to walk. Reluctantly we all set off for our homes. The weather was great for a mid-June evening, and although it was a little muggy, there was no sign of rain. I walked and smiled thinking about our family and how my mother had rebounded after my father's death to still give us a great life."

"I was almost home, probably three blocks from my apartment, when I saw seven to ten young men running towards me. I thought nothing of this as groups of young people we're always seem together in large numbers."

"Young people loved to walk and laugh in the streets. They quickly painted graffiti on the walls, so as to not get caught, and learned to smoke cigarettes together. These were daily daily occurrences, but unfortunately not that night."

"One of the boys grabbed my right arm before I even knew what happened. He slammed me into another boy, and they were screaming something at each other in another language that I did not recognize."

"Later I would find out that it was Arabic. Two of the boys picked me up by my legs and they all proceeded to carry me like I was a prized animal in a stockyard. "

"Another one of the boys covered my mouth so that I couldn't scream and they hauled me into an alley between two garbage cans. It was dark and I could not see their faces when the streetlights would shine I know they had dark eyes and dark hair."

"They had come from another country but I didn't know which one. Everything happened so fast. A couple of the boys were ripping off my top and my bra in the second set of boys were ripping off my jeans and my shoes."

Nadja was beginning to get uncomfortable, sick to her stomach and started to cry, she forced herself to continue to listen. Someone else had suffered and she didn't feel so all alone. After all, Elza wasn't even Yezidi. She needed to hear from start to finish what made Elza who she was.

A strong and caring individual isn't just born, but has been transformed though many fires and this was one she needed to share in. The sufferings of another could change the listener because she knew in her heart that the outcome had to be more profound than those painful moments shared.

Elza continued, "At that point I was squirming and trying to get away, but they held a tight grip on me. I couldn't believe I had come from such a wonderful time with my family and then I was about to be raped by hellish fiends. I kept trying to think slowly or quickly, it didn't matter, on how to get away."

"My mind was totally blank and I had not had enough time to be afraid. I just kept thinking that what was happening couldn't be my reality after such a wonderful day. I knew that there just had to be some way to get away. That is when I heard my panties tear away from body."

"I was totally naked in an alley between two garbage cans and with my mouth covered by one of their dirty hands, there was almost no sound. They worked feverishly like they were on smoking of mission."

"They were all determined to take a part of me that I could never retrieve. There was a sense that they have done this before as they worked methodically and without remorse. Not one stopped the other."

"Then I felt fingers pinch my breasts, enter my vagina and my anus all at the same time. I went into shock. Then without any warning one sprang on top of me and entered my body with a painful stab. I was laying on my back on the hard ground and it didn't matter to the boy that as he pushed me into the rocks, I was being cut."

"When he was finished he looked at me and scream something and then the next one proceeded to take his turn. He was more vicious than the first and he pulled my hair and screamed while he raped me."

"On and on they went, while some took two turns and some even took three. I was bleeding and exhausted and at that point I could only pray that they would not kill me. It was only when they became so tired that they could not go on they took turns beating me. I was hit and kicked until I was unconscious."

"My last conscious thought was my concern for them. It was not anger, but their lack of any compassion for another human being. I wanted to let them know that there was another way. A way out of there abject darkness."

"And at that point I remember nothing more. Everything went black and the darkness that surrounded me truly was the mercy of God. I so wanted to escape the horrible onslaught in that alley that night and when my lights went out I considered that a perfect retreat."

"A neighbor had found me in the morning when her dog began to bark at something moving by the trash dumpster. She wept as she called the police and an ambulance. Her little dog and I had become good friends, and had he not sensed my distress I made not have been here to tell you my story. We never know who will be there in our darkest hours. God truly works in mysterious ways."

Elza went on. "I woke up in the hospital several days later unable to see or speak. I had been sedated so that I couldn't move. They had beat me until my eyes were swollen shut. I could not find my voice as it was lost way down in the pits of my anguish."

"I heard the voices of my family, but most of all I heard my mother writhing in anguish as she stood over my bed. She was unconsolable. I felt her hot tears falling on my hand but I could not speak."

"The doctor entered the room and asked if they could step outside. I knew things were bad because he did not even want to speak in the same hospital room where I laid. I knew that things were bad but I no idea how bad."

"Later I would find out that I had several ribs broken along with a broken arm that was fractured in three places. My facial bones were completely shattered the right side."

"These bones were replaced by bones from hips. Along with this, they had broken both of my pelvic bones, and I would find out that I had contracted a rare form of Gonorrhea that the doctors were trying to treat."

Nadja was trying to compose herself. She had no idea that behind Elza's smile was a woman who had experienced such terrible human tragedy on such a deep personal level. She held everyone else together each day and even into the nights, when the demons were unleashed in the dark.

There were no words to comfort either one of them. Neither one of them desired to be consoled, but finally set free from the grip of their memories. The flood of tears unleashed an assault on the chains that held them invisibly, but were strong, none the less.

Elza was older than Nadja by a decade, but Nadja's experiences had brought her into an prolific understanding of human nature in its darkest and lowest stages. Elza had experienced and traveled down an agonizing path, but something within her refused to bargain with the demons that drove those young men on the night that changed her life.

She had examined this precious woman's life, and came to the conclusion that she wanted what Elza had. She flew like a bird with no more apparent chains.

First she had a freedom to talk about what had transpired on that fateful evening. She was giving everyone a gift that crossed her path. Permission to take another step. It was from the depths of her soul.

She also, was shameless and free from her captors and Nadja desired this more than anything. Nadja realized that her rapists still controlled her very thoughts and ultimately her actions. even though they were miles away.

Nadja had some choice decisions to make. She had been through some terrible things in her young life, but she had to evaluate the options realistically. She could hold on to the shame, or let it fly away and set it free.

She would have to grow old with the memories taking total control, or choose to take control over her own future. Her life was in her own hands, or some unseen force that could guide her through this ugly mental maze.

The next questions were asked in total silence. Elza knew all along that Nadja was mystified. Nadja, after all had heard bits and pieces that no one else had been privy to. Elza had pulled out all the stops in an effort to get Nadja to respond.

It had worked and now Nadja was engulfed in a stream of tears. Her tears told her story. She wanted out of her prison of pain and loneliness.

FIGHTING BACK

She could not change her past, but she could do plenty about her future and there was someone standing right beside her that could assist in her quest.

Nadja had really heard Elza. She had relived each moment that Elza had so painfully described. she felt the grip of the arms that had restrained Elza. She had experienced the anger in every kick and broken bone that Elza had suffered.

Yet, Elza had spoken of this one night of horror so calmly. The shame and disgrace were replaced with a love and empathy for her assailants. It was almost unsettling the way that Elza detached herself from the brutality that she had suffered.

She almost spoke as if it had happened to someone else. But there was no doubt in Nadja's mind that Elza was giving her each and every detail with a firm conviction that it would resonate with Nadja.

Elza stood motionless. There was even more to say. She knew that the time had come to bring Nadja to the point of making some hard decisions. They would speak to each other woman to woman. There would be an intense reality check because Nadja's life step ended on it and Elza knew it.

Nadja simply had to know, what made Elza persevere. That this new step would take everything in her and more. She too had lived and lost. Nadja had mistakingly perceived her life as carefree, and that of a woman who had no worries or past.

It was time to know the deep mysteries centered around Elza's joy and contentment. There was no way that this lovely woman could fake her balanced personality. She simply could not keep up her positive flow if it were not there.

Nadja began to probe Elza. She was ready to ask the questions that would cut her wide open and cause the healing to flow. She would accept the answers whatever they would be.

Nadja knew that the end of Elza's story was to come. She had not arrived at a conclusion to press onward with so many emotional strings hanging. "Is there more?", Nadja asked Elza

Elza continued her story, and it would not be told the way Nadja had expected. Elza began to describe the days that followed. Day after day her life had gotten extremely hard. She was searching from a bed at her mother's home to find meaning. And then things really took a turn for the worse.

Elsa did not come out of the hospital whoever thinking that life was gong to be magically delicious. She suffered deep trauma and the physical pain was almost more than she could bear.

Elza's mother had to rush her to the hospital as she was ravished with intolerable pain. Infection had set into her uterus and her ovaries. She was so discouraged and ready to give up.

The doctors could not figure out how to treat the infection so she was immediately carted off to surgery where she was dispensed a massive hysterectomy. and her dreams of having children was over. She was shattered. This was not a life that she would have chosen for her worst enemy, if she had any.

She had to be given intravenous transfusions of antibiotics. This was literally to save her life. She was bed ridden and completely helpless. She was lost in a world of pain pills and sedatives with life swimming around her as a deep ocean.

On top of all this, she was reliving time and time again the gang rape, coupled with imaginary voices. There was a laughter from hell, and scowls for a woman they abhorred just because she was different from them. There were other hideous sounds that played in her mind as if it was all reoccurring.

She could not reach the pain medication that she had been prescribed. She had decided to place each new tablet in her drawer. She started spitting them out as fast as they were giving them to her. Her body may have felt some relief, but her mind was playing dark tricks on her.

But at that moment, she had wanted them all. She could have ended the jeers and mocking forever, if she could just take as many pills as she could get down her throat to end it all. She could not see her life past the pain of knowing she had been used lie a dirty rag. She just wanted to end it all.

Nadja listened and could not believe her ears. Elza was at that point ready to take her own life. Nadja remembered her mother and how she had refused to live in slavery another day. She would tell Elza about there other, but not now. She would wait until a later time.

Elza continued speaking about her willingness to let go of her own life, as she felt the grip of too many past ghosts. She had tried to think of one reason there was to go go on living….she couldn't come up with one.

Then the miraculous occurred. As Elza had laid in her bed, begging for death, a hospital staff woman entered the room. Elza could see the she was a foreigner, but didn't tax herself about what country the woman may be from. Perhaps somewhere in Asia. She didn't know.

Then the woman opened her mouth and the sweetest sound came out that Elza had ever heard. She sang gently under her breath as she straighten up the room. She ignored Elza and made herself busy taking inventory of what would be needed in the room.

Elza stated that she, herself, had initiated the conversation. The woman kept singing and Elza thought that the woman could not understand German. Elza spoke English, and a little French. She would go on to learn to be fluent in Kumanji Kurdish so as to make the women feel more at home.

But this woman who had entered her room seemed strange and not aware that Elza was at the end of her life's rope. Elza spoke to her but the woman, just stared at her and then opened up her mouth and laughter poured out.

Elza was totally confused at this point and asked the woman to leave. She came closer to the bed and Elza saw that she had a name tag on that read, "Aashi". Elza would find out that this name means "Smile" in Hindu. This woman was from India.

The woman took both s Elza's hands. She looked up and said nothing other than, "Jesus". She began to sob. She spoke in English that she was taking "the men" away from her forever. She wept like Elza was her very own child. Elza then began to weep too.

The woman gently let go of Elza's hands and covered her feet. She backed out of the room like a humble servant paying homage to a queen. In a moment she was gone.

Elza looked at her hands and they came into focus. She checked her body and she was astounded that all of her pain was gone. Elza could not describe a what had happened to her other than she had taken some sort of spiritual bath.

Elza was released from the hospital a few days later with her doctors in astonishment. She was healed from all of the infection that had placed her there.

Then it happened. She was saying good bye to many of the staff memes who had helped her in so many ways. Her eyes searched for the woman by the name of Aashi. She didn't see her anywhere on her floor in the lobby.

Elza asked if she could be wheeled to the reception desk and there she would ask for the woman to come to her so she could give her thanks and a big hug. She didn't know how to put it into words, but she was grateful none the less.

Elza told Nadja how she had requested to see this lady before she would leave the hospital. Many people who worked at the reception desk. But, all the staff agreed that there had never been anyone employed there with that name in that particular hospital. In fact, there was no one there at that time from India, not even a doctor.

Elza referred to her as, "her angel" and said that she owed every smile to this woman and Jesus as long as she would live…and live she did.

CHAPTER TEN

"BEGINNINGS"

"We must accept finite disappointment, but never lose infinite hope"

Dr. Martin Luther King, Jr.

Nadja is only one of about 1,000 girls who had escaped ISIS captivity. No one really know the numbers of captives or those who fled to safety. No one really knows how many were killed while in captive.

They were nameless and faceless both world and would remain that way because of Yezedi traditions and possibly the collective apathy, that occurs in nations that have a chronic history of wars

Unlike the Nazis, ISIS did not keep track of their victims. They were prone to execute their captives on videos, but none of them recorded the exterminations or the kidnappings.

This may have been because the ISIS camps were disorganized, many possibly questioning leadership, and many other members were from various countries. They had been either killed or brutalized almost beyond repair. Suicides were off the chart as many women could not cope with the lingering fears or memories.

After being taken to freedom by Amir and the other Peshmerga soldiers, Nadja held a real hope in her heart, but doubt filled her mind that she would ever see her younger brother or sister ever again. She knew that they would be mentally mutilated for the rest of their life.

Each one of the children, through no fault of their own had become different human beings. How could her younger brother be drugged, fed alcohol and kill on the front lines and be anything else but different?

Nadja had been one of the fortunate to be found and brought to a place where she could begin healing. She was desperate to begin to feel again. Nadja was brought to Sege after she had been taken to the Temple in Lalish to be bathed for purification.

The Elders of the Yezidi Community tried to give these precious children hope through a ritual bathing. They wanted to reinforce the notion that they were still Yezidi and welcomed. However, she could never marry or have a family of her own. She was scrubbed with oils and spices, but this did nothing for her Nadja's mind or soul.

The memories were even fresher and more bitter. She had escaped but she could not escape the feel of the hands and the grip of their lewdness. This place was for the repair of souls, not merely surviving their personal holocaust, but entirely rebuilding their lives. Each girl had right to live and tell the world what is happening in Kurdistan and many places in IRAQ.

Nadja's mind kept traveling back to the good times and she was reminded of that special day in the village right before she had arrived in Germany. See was residing in a little village trying to breathe.

She had been brought there by Amir not only because it was a Christian village, but homes and lives were opened up to the surviving Yezidis. She had been able to come and be with other Yezidi people who understood some of her pain following her rescue.

Nadja had learned, however, in the last several months to stop verbally complaining about any of her past or present circumstances. It did no good. She was looking at lives that were so destroyed that she couldn't believe they were even still part of living.

There were several women living in the clinic who were on the brink of losing their very minds. They moped, cried and wandered through each day. Nadja could still formulate her thoughts, her desires and what she hoped would lead to an amazing future now that she was free from the animals.

FREEDOM

The rain had finally stopped. She was relieved. To Nadja this was a sign. Maybe she would venture out. No, she would leave her den of memories and head for a fresher environment.

Nadja had looked forward to seeing Elza each day, because she was pure and consistent in her efforts. Nadja had searched Elza's motives and now it was time to search her own heart. She saw nothing that would stand in the way of her being restored to at least to some degree,

Elza was a warrior for peace and love. Elsa would be a great teacher as time went on because she had been on the battlefield. She was calm but her quick and firm decisions, in the way that she intuitively worked with the women, brought such a deep sense of respect. She would not be defeated and moreover, she expected results and healing where the women were concerned.

Nadja knew that Elza knew who she was as a person. It wasn't that she didn't have fears, she had spoken of them. She just refused to release them release them on anyone else, because of her strong discipline.

She cared more about the well-being of the suffering women then she did about her own past experiences. It was though she could rise to the occasion to assist with the emotional bandages of the women at a moments notice.

There was now a brand new resolve in her that would not allow victimization. Elza had refused to bow down to the demented men that characterized themselves as people and so would she.

She would have children just like Elza, even if they didn't come from her body. She would have more children than any physically healthy woman could imagine. They would come from near and far and they would be rescued to set the world on fire with love.

Nadja wanted to return to the joys of childhood, but she was broken in places that she never even realized that she had, but she was determined to gain some kind of solace. She had begun to embrace this opportunity with that many women, who had been taken as slaves, would never even get the chance to experience.

Nadja thought quietly to herself, "I am going to try the thing called, 'life' just one more time. Something or someone has caused a new hope to spring in her heart, and she would not have to walk to the beat of a hollow rhythm. "Look at Elza", she thought, she did not stop dreaming of becoming.

She had robbed those animals of the power over her future that they had terrorized her for just one dark night. Nadja would not allow it either. She would not be like those men who had ravished and stolen her youth. She was not ever going to be changed into them, hate filled and merciless.

This time she could hear Elza's words like never before. "May I get you **anything**, Nadja?" She was also getting enough courage to ask questions of her own. Nadja had been initiated into an experience that few women would ever go through or ever understand.

The tone in her soft voice had a much different ring. Nadja marked Elza's words and her question took on a profound ring. She had managed to hear the soft words that were drowning out the screams of her not so distant past.

Now in some small way she was very determined to find her own voice again. She chose to rise above her pain to breathe again, and was determined to begin some hope of a new life at least for her shattered family's sake.

Nadja wanted with all that was left of her heart, for every woman to know how abuse looks when it dresses up behind religion or racism to show itself, and the ravished angels left behind in its horrid path. She was now more determined than ever to use her own prison to see as many women set free who had suffered the same horrors.

Silently she sought to see others healed who stood motionless and who had been caught in the fray of sheer barbarism. They weren't mentally back yet from the grips of their captors and some would never mentally regain even one day of a normal existence.

Nadja wanted to face the world. She sat quietly on the sofa in the longe. She would not return to her room to hide out. She sat patiently and waited for Elza to return from seeing one of the other women.

When Elza arrived she asked Elza to sit with her because she had something that she wanted to tell her. Elza sat down beside her and without another word she took Nadja's hands in her own. Nadja knew that Elza knew.

When Elza looked up, everything seemed to culminate into one moment. Elza quietly said the Name of Jesus and every memory that Nadja had ever experienced seem to flood her mind. She was forgiving every captor, every rapist, every neighbor who had betrayed their families. Nadja was being set free and she knew it. She was letting them all go.

She was given a certain ritualistic permission from her own people. Maybe the Baba Sheikh was right at the holy site of Lalish. He was so tender and agreed not to ostracize the victims, despite the perceived affront to having lost all honor in their culture. They all had been victims of terrible crimes perpetrated on them by forces so evil.

Nadja began to share parts of her story with others who had suffered the same ordeal. When she arrived, however she was drawn to one young Yezidi girl in particular, who was just one year older than herself. She had been in the safety of the same village that Nadja was sent from, but they had not previous met.

Sege, in Kurdistan, was a drop off point until the girls could get someone to send them to Germany or to another place of safety. Many young women were coming to this village instead of going to the camps, where many times, by night, they were raped all over again.

Nadja had felt such a deep sorrow for the young girl that she had met. The girls had only been there for two weeks when she imagined that she had heard the voices of Islamic State fighters outside her home.

She was so frightened by the thought of being raped and abused at their hands again, and she had promised to make herself so undesirable that they would never again even look at her. So, like so many others, she doused herself in gasoline and then lit a match. The flames burned her hair and face, burning away her nose, lips and ears.

This was a constant in the lives of the young girls who had suffered and yet, there was no real escaping the recent memories. Someone in the village had passed the word along that this girl was so mutilated, both physically and psychologically, that they begged help for her.

When Nadja asked her about her painful experiences, she just shakes and trembles and grab the edge of her chair. Her main concern is that someone from ISIS welcome back and repeat the same tortures and she lives gripped in fear.

Another girl shared her heartbreaking story. One of the girls shared how she was separated from all the others and brought to several places so as to confuse her about her destination. She was then dropped off at the home of a certain Syrian family.

She was already pregnant and, of course, her husband had been killed in Sinjar. She also had other little children with her. Some of them were hers, and others were children that had been rescued during the invasion. She shared how the people that she ended up with were very cruel to her and the children.

She was beaten daily in spite of the fact that she was pregnant. She was hit while she was being raped by various family members. If she refused to have sex with these men, they would hold her down, and all take their turn raping and hitting her.

After being sold again, this time to a family from Saudi Arabia, they took one of the boys who was with her to be trained as a Jihadi. She will never see him again.

She stayed there for one month and a half and then moved again, to another home, where my baby was born. She was raped there too repeatedly despite the fact that she had just given birth.

The stories went on and on. Many talked about how they were afraid to wash because the rapes would be even more numerous. Some were beat if they reluctantly agreed to the violent sexual attacks just for the sake of survival.

Oddly enough, by visiting the lives of others and facing her own personal hell, Nadja had been strangely liberated. Yet, Nadja didn't feel sorry for herself for one moment. She had been like a little bird with both wings broken from a pushed fall. However, now she did not think for one moment that she would never fly again.

MIRACLES

Elza spoke to Nadja of miracles. But it was hard to constitute in one's mind the idea of the impossible when so much of her reality made her doubt most things about life.

Nadja was being released from the darkness in incremental steps and all of this was because she had been introduced to "the Light".

Her heart was beginning to define hope, and she was slowly being introduced to the concept of forgiveness. She may one day receive the greatest gift of all, freedom through forgiveness for the very vilest of characters.

Forgiveness was slowly and remarkably cleansing her soul from every rape and assault that she had suffered for almost one year of her young life. As those chains were breaking, and she never wanted to return to those awful pits of bondage and despair again.

She knew that if she didn't embark on facing all of her recent past with bravery and honor, she would be haunted by the real emery, one more dangerous than all of ISIS….herself. She had the keys to unlock every painful door, she just had use them and begin to look into every one. Just behind the doors was a new life, a life that could help others just like Elza had helped her.

As people sang and spoke around the piano, the music was like a long lost friend. All the new people were being greeted. They had brought in a few young girls who were rescued from Mosul. Nadja looked for her sister and brother to come into the facility everyday, and her heart was so heavy when neither arrived.

Then the impossible happened. At first Nadja didn't see her. Many were the same age as Nasima. But then she stopped and looked at the children closer. "Could it be?", thought Nadja. Her heart had played ticks on her before. Could it be possible that she would be able to hold her little sister again?

A slight glimpse under the direct the direct lights revealed that one of her dreams had come true. Nadja got up and ran to Nasima in the hallway. She was afraid to hug her knowing how she felt when she was finally rescued by Amir. Touch was the last thing that she needed right now.

It was her alright, but it was not her at all. It was someone who had taken over the body of a small, beautiful, and innocent child. One that had once been so full of laughter and life.

This was Nasima's body alright, but another little girl possessed her. Her eyes were dark and her smile was gone. Her little sister, Nasima had been raped as a small child and lived to be raped again repeatedly by those who paid the highest price for a very young girl. Nadja had thought that she had been killed, for some reason, but the fact was Nasima had been sold over and over again.

It made virtually made no difference that she was just a small child, and only as old as the children that she had cleaned up behind in the homes of the strangers. She was sold as a sex slave to a fighter from Yeman, and then she was sold over and over again the next year.

At 11 years old, she had been forced to do things that no grown-up woman could imagine. Regardless, Nadja could sense that she was experiencing the very thing that Elza kept speaking to her heart about. One day the God of the Christians would make himself known to her in a real way.

It was her, but she did not readily recognize Nadja. Perhaps she thought that she was seeing a ghost. She was so traumatized that she could not speak or respond to any words.

All that mattered in that time and place was that Nadja had found her sister. It didn't matte the condition as she was still alive. She was a little living vegetable who had been freed when Mosul was attacked. She was passed around like a rag doll from one soldier to another. From one buyer to another for over a year.

Little Nasima had scars and burns all over her arms and legs and it was apparent that she had been beaten, abused and finally abandoned. Nadja was secretly glad that Rooba did not have to witness the remnant of what had been left of her child.

As Nadja began slowly to try and restore life to Nasima, she could see the light grow in her little sister's eyes. It was as if Nasima was a gift to help Nadja grow in spite of all that had happened to her and her family. God had stopped the entire universe to come and see about her and Nasima. Nadja was a part of the impossible and she knew it.

She swore on the death of her mother and father that she would care for Nasima all the days of her life. But this would be an undertaking that she would not be able to do alone. She began to look up and to cry out. May the God of the Christians help me, please.

Suddenly Nadja just wanted to heal others through her story. "It is very important to tell our stories because the world should know what happened to us, so that it doesn't happen again," she says. Maybe this would shake the Western World to see what the weapons left behind in Baghdad had done.

She even thought that one day she may want to see America, but now she believed that America needed to see her.

ABOUT THE AUTHOR

Barb is currently residing and working in Kurdistan, Northern Region of IRAQ, as the Owner of the Dream Center Language Institute. She has served the Global Community Teaching Leadership Training, Entrepreneurial Building, and as a teacher in various other subjects. Through her efforts she has consistently worked for the betterment of humankind.

She has traveled to the People's Democratic Republic of Congo on several occasions, Uganda, Rwanda, Ethiopia and Somalia in Eastern Africa. She has had the privilege of meeting with many Government Leaders. Barb has also successfully owned and managed two businesses, while serving and volunteering in her local community in the United States of America.

She has taught Leadership and Successful Life Skills for over twenty years. She has worked to establish confidence, courage, and inspiration for those who dare to dream. She has succeeded, both as a paid Professional Consultant and as an English Teacher.

She has been a United States Congressional Candidate, for the 5th District of Minnesota twice, and she is also a Licensed and Ordained Pastor, holding a Masters Degree in Theological Studies from Bethel Seminary, in St. Paul, Minnesota.

Made in the USA
Lexington, KY
07 May 2018